Holocaust Memories

Holocaust Memories

A Survey of Holocaust Memoirs, Histories, Novels, and Films

Claudia Moscovici

Foreword by Rabbi Joseph Polak

Hamilton Books
Lanham • Boulder • New York • Toronto • London

Published by Hamilton Books
An imprint of The Rowman & Littlefield Publishing Group, Inc.
4501 Forbes Boulevard, Suite 200, Lanham, Maryland 20706
Hamilton Books Acquisitions Department (301) 459-3366

6 Tinworth Street, London SE11 5AL

Copyright © 2019 by The Rowman & Littlefield Publishing Group, Inc.

All rights reserved. No part of this book may be produced in any form or by any electronic means, including information storage and retrieval systems, without written permission from the publisher, except by a reviewer who may quote passages in a review.

British Library Cataloguing in Publication Information Available

Library of Congress Control Number: 2019937969

ISBN 978-0-7618-7092-0 (pbk.)
ISBN 978-0-7618-7093-7 (electronic)

To my parents, Henri and Elvira Moscovici, and in loving memory of my grandparents, Sara and Avram Moscovici and Eszter and Ion Buzulica

Contents

Foreword	ix
Preface: A Precedent for the Holocaust: The Armenian Genocide and The Promise	xi
Introduction	1
1 Between Fanaticism and Terror: Hitler, Stalin, and The Noise of Time	5
2 Elie Wiesel's Night: Shedding Light upon the Darkness	9
3 Bergen-Belsen and Four Perfect Pebbles	13
4 The Last Seven Months of Anne Frank by Willy Lindwer	17
5 Hazy Hints of Memory: After the Holocaust the Bells Still Ring	19
6 Survivors Club: A Family's Legendary Tale	23
7 Primo Levi's Reflection on Humanity in Crisis: Survival in Auschwitz	27
8 Sarah's Key and the Holocaust in France	31
9 The Holocaust in Hungary: Leni Yahil's The Holocaust	33
10 A Holocaust Hero in Hungary: Wallenberg by Kati Marton	35
11 Imre Kertesz's Fatelessness	39
12 Anti-Semitism in Hungary Today	41
13 Hannah Arendt's The Origins of Totalitarianism: Why the Jews?	43
14 The Role of the Masses in The Origins of Totalitarianism	47
15 Beyond the Jewish Genocide: Inferno by Max Hastings	51
16 Hitler's Ban on Modern Art: The "Degenerate Art" Exhibit	53

17	Saving European Art from the Nazis: The Monuments Men	55
18	The Holocaust in Austria and Woman in Gold	59
19	On the Anschluss: Becoming Alice	61
20	The Gypsy Holocaust: The Nazi Persecution of the Gypsies	63
21	Eichmann in Jerusalem: What is the Banality of Evil?	65
22	The Real Banality of Evil: Ordinary Men by Christopher R. Browning	71
23	Eichmann's Extraordinary Evil: Eichmann Before Jerusalem	73
24	The Concentration Camp Commandants: Soldiers of Evil	77
25	The Auschwitz Kommandant: Arthur Wilhelm Liebehenschel	81
26	The Real Story of the Terezin Jewish Ghetto: I Am a Star	85
27	The Wannsee Conference: Planning the Final Solution	89
28	America First	91
29	Quiet Neighbors by Allan A. Ryan	95
30	Action T4: From "Euthanasia" to the Final Solution	97
31	Hitler's Niece and Historical Fiction	101
32	An Unlikely Hero: Schindler's List by Thomas Keneally	105
33	The Boy in the Striped Pajamas: An Instructive Fable	109
34	Forgiven but Never Forgotten	113
35	The 1936 Berlin Olympics: The Boys in the Boat	117
36	Manufacturing Death: Hell's Cartel	119
37	Prosecuting War Crimes: The Nuremberg Trial	123
38	Kamikaze Warfare: Inferno	127
39	Hateful Words: Nazi Propaganda	129
40	A Cowardly Success: Bloodlands	133
41	Planning a Soviet Holocaust: Stalin's Last Crime	135
42	Lebensraum: The Second World War	139
43	The Siege of Leningrad and Genocide by Starvation	141
44	The Murderous Einsatzgruppen (Task Forces): Israel Gutman's Resistance	143
45	Poland's Plight: Gustaw Herling's A World Apart	147
46	Children of the War Years: Witnesses of War	149
47	Sophie's Choice: Holocaust Literature as Psychological Fiction	151
48	An Incredible Tale of Survival: Alicia: My Story	155
49	Revealing the Ugly Truth: The Holocaust in Romania	157

50 A Romanian Hero: The Memoirs of Wilhelm Filderman	161
51 Ion Antonescu: Hitler's Forgotten Ally	163
52 Anti-Semitism in Romania: The Journal of Mihai Sebastian	167
53 Heroism in Hell: Resistance: The Warsaw Ghetto Uprising	171
54 Privilege and Persecution: The Diary of Mary Berg	175
55 Janusz Korczak: The King of the Children of the Warsaw Ghetto	177
56 The Pianist: The Extraordinary Story of Survival in Warsaw	179
57 Trapped in the Lodz Ghetto: The Cage	181
58 The Book Thief: Holocaust Literature as Best Seller	185
59 The Forgotten Holocaust: The Rape of Nanking	187
60 A Cataclysmic War: Postwar: A History of Europe since 1945	189
61 The Cultural Revolution and the Great Leap Forward	191
62 The Killing Fields: Genocide in Cambodia	195
63 Genocide in Rwanda: Me Against My Brother	197
64 North Korea's State of Terror: Nothing to Envy	201
65 Yad Vashem: "A Place and a Name" of Remembrance	205
66 An Impossible Conflict in Gaza: Rock the Casbah	209
67 Anti-Semitism Today and the Assault on Democratic Values	213
68 Would You Forgive the Nazi Perpetrator?: The Sunflower	215
69 Could the Holocaust Happen Again?: Nazi Hunter	219
70 Ethics above Politics	221
Conclusion: Judaic Studies and the Holocaust via Reviews	223
Bibliography	227
About the Author	231

Foreword

This book, full of considerations of the unbearable, is haunted by a question posed, but never fully articulated by the author, along the following lines: How is it that I am so drawn to the Holocaust and its ensuing literature, especially as I was born so many years after 1945? Why am I somehow so intuitively familiar with it, with its darkness and its cold, its choiceless choices, its helplessness?

It is an amazing work not just for its considerable breadth and scholarship, but because in the enormity of its range, in its drive, in the unyielding brutality of its subject matter, the author never fails to write her essays with anything but the highest discipline and deepest scholarly calm. The book's moral outrage, manifest on every page, is delivered between the lines, perhaps by its very thoroughness. Yet it also provokes a second disturbing question—what part of her soul seeks satisfaction, needs answers, from all this?

It has to do, it seems to me, with being raised in Romania, behind the iron curtain, in the shadow of what Stalin had wrought, his murders more numerous than Hitler's, and from the helplessness that comes from living in a regime where your activities are not constrained by your own values but by those of Big Brother. There is humiliation that comes from having lived in, and thereby unwillingly acceded to, a morally compromised society, and this humiliation, far from going away as the years move on, begs for resolution.

Claudia Moscovici is not the first scholar to face this challenge. Hannah Arendt left Europe when the maelstrom had already begun, surely offended, and ultimately deeply humiliated by her relationship not just with her teacher Heidegger, but with the intellectual heights of German culture that had so finely nurtured her, and that had in the end, so unforgivingly betrayed her.

Arendt, the subject of more essays here than anyone else, is omnipresent in this book. Moscovici is talking about her when she is ostensibly talking about Eichmann, she is talking about her when she speaks of Stagneth; in fact, I suspect that she is talking about Arendt whenever she introduces concepts of evil in every one of these essays, asking, without always articulating it—"Banality?—is this what characterizes evil? Really?"

Arendt attended a limited number of the sessions of Eichmann's trial, and was always in the press room and never in the court room when she did, so it is not clear that she actually saw the man falsely claiming to be just following orders, nor certainly that she had the opportunity to study Eichmann long enough, like an artist gazing at his model, to judge him banal. Arendt, in a tasteless moment, chose to blame the victims ("sheep to slaughter") of the Holocaust, rather than to excoriate the behavior of its key perpetrator (Eichmann). This is Arendt, I believe, coping badly with her own humiliation by the Third Reich and its intellectuals.

Not so our author, who it seems, has heard other, more mature voices. She manages to find in Arendt the closest understanding yet about how Auschwitz and the Gulag mirror each other, and learned from Arendt's writing, if not from her example, how to talk about the two in the same breath without compromising and without diminishing either one.

The screen that portrays the horrors of the twentieth Century is fading more rapidly than its audience can bear. Claudia Moscovici's book will go far to help keep it lit longer.

Rabbi Joseph Polak
Author of *After the Holocaust the Bells Still Ring*
Winner of the 2015 National Jewish Book Award
Boston, December, 2016

Preface

*A Precedent for the Holocaust:
The Armenian Genocide and The Promise*

As Peter Balakian points out in the Preface of his book, *The Burning Tigris: The Armenian Genocide and America's Response* (New York: Harper Perennial, 2004), the Holocaust had a significant historical precedent: one which, unfortunately, is all too often ignored. The Armenian genocide, he states, "has often been referred to as 'the forgotten genocide,' 'the unremembered genocide,' 'the hidden holocaust,' or 'the secret genocide'" (xvii). He adds that many historians—including Yehuda Bauer, Robert Melson, Howard M. Sachar and Samantha Power—rightfully consider the Armenian genocide to be "the template for most of the genocide that followed in the twentieth century" (xviii).

Over a century later, Turkey still refuses to acknowledge the systematic and premeditated mass killings of the Armenian population by the Ottoman Turks, even though this genocide, officially recognized as such by twenty-nine countries, is well documented: "In the past two decades, scholars have unearthed and translated a large quantity of official state records documenting the Committee of Union and Progress's (Ottoman Turkey's governing political party) finely organized and Implemented plan to exterminate the Armenians" (xxi). Balakian himself studied "hundreds of U.S. State Department documents (there are some four thousand documents totaling about thirty-seven thousand pages in the National Archives) written by American diplomats that report in-depth the process and devastation of the Armenian Genocide. The extermination of the Armenians is also illuminated in British Foreign Office records, and in official records from the state archives of Germany and Austria-Hungary, Ottoman Turkey's World War I allies. The foremost scholar of the Armenian Genocide, Professor Vahakn Dadrian, has made available in translation the body of Turkish sources both primary and secondary" (xxi).

The genocide involved the systematic mass murder and ethnic cleansing of approximately 1.5 million Armenians by the Ottoman Turks during World War I. The extermination started on April 24, 1915, with the deportation and execution of a few hundred Armenian intellectuals from Constantinople. It progressed to the forced conscription, imprisonment in labor camps and murder of able-bodied males. Soon thereafter, it led to the mass murder of women, the elderly and children, who were herded by Turkish military escorts for hundreds of miles across the Syrian desert, without sufficient food, water, medical care or sanitary facilities. The Turks butchered entire villages and communities mercilessly driven on these death marches. Women and young girls were often subjected to rape and torture before being killed. Sometimes the victims were loaded on cattle trains for days, without any provisions, in a manner similar to the Nazi transportation of Jews to concentration camps almost three decades later.

Similarly to the Jewish Holocaust, the Armenian Holocaust didn't happen out of the blue. Like the Jews in many European countries, the Armenians were considered second-class citizens in the Ottoman Empire. Even during relatively Enlightened times, when the Ottoman rulers granted the Christian and Jewish minorities some autonomy and minority rights, non-Muslims were still considered to be "gavours," meaning "infidels" or "unbelievers." In the Eastern provinces, Armenian villages found themselves subject to higher taxation and often invaded by their Turkish and Kurdish neighbors. Moreover, like the Jews in the Pale of Settlement region, the Armenians fell victim to periodic pogroms.

However, discrimination and subjugation don't necessarily lead to widescale genocide. Consequently, just as the Jews couldn't have anticipated the extermination of their people by the Nazis, nothing prepared the Armenian communities living under Ottoman rule for their ethnic cleansing at the hands of the Turks. In both cases, world wars were used as an excuse—and incitement—for genocide. The Ottoman Empire entered WWI on August 2, 1914, when it signed a secret treaty with Germany to fight on the side of the Axis powers. The Turkish leadership wanted the local Armenian population to act on their behalf, demanding their insurrection against the Russian Army. The Minister of War, Enver Pasha, launched an attack on the Russians. He attempted to encircle and destroy the Russian army at Sarikamish in order to reclaim the Turkish territories occupied by the Russians since 1877. However, his plan failed and his troops were defeated. The Turks blamed their loss on the local Armenian population, viewing them as traitors who helped the Russians. Subsequently, able-bodied Armenian men living in the Ottoman Empire were discharged from active military service, disarmed, and sent to forced labor battalions, where many were executed by the Turks.

In a move that would prefigure the Jewish genocide in the Eastern Territories during WWII, on May 29, 2015, the Turkish Central Committee passed a law of deportation (called the "Tehcir Law") that gave the Ottoman Empire the right to deport anyone they considered a threat to "national security," which, in their estimation, included women and children. The mass deportation—in grueling death marches—of the elderly, women and children soon followed. Hundreds of thousands of Armenians died from starvation, disease, and mass shootings. To carry out the genocide, the Turks formed a paramilitary organization that has been compared by historians to the Nazi Einsatzgruppen. The Turkish Committee of Union and Progress founded a "Special Organization," comprised mostly of Turkish criminals released from prisons, who were put in charge of the deportations and massacres of the Armenians. They killed countless helpless civilians, decimating their numbers through forced marches, shootings, mass burning, drowning, and even poisoning. Like the Nazis, the Turks experimented with toxic gases and biological warfare (by inoculating healthy Armenians with the blood of typhoid patients). After the Allies defeated the Axis powers, on November 3, 1918, Sultan Mehmet VI was ordered by the Allied administration to hold war trials for the Turkish leaders of the Armenian genocide, which included Mehmed Talaat Pasha, Enver Pasha and about 130 high officials of the Ottoman Empire.

The film *The Promise* (2016), directed by Terry George, captures the trauma of the Armenian genocide in an epic drama reminiscent of *War and Peace*. The movie traces a love triangle between Mikael, an Armenian medical student, and Ana, an Armenian tutor educated in France, who is in turn engaged to Chris, an American journalist covering the war for the Associated Press. A small town boy from a poor family, before meeting Ana, Mikael himself becomes engaged to a wealthier neighbor, whose family gives him a dowry (400 gold coins) to cover his expenses for medical school in Constantinople. At a party held by his wealthy uncle, Mikael is introduced to Ana, his nieces' tutor, as well as Emre, the son of a Turkish official, whom he befriends. He's smitten with Ana as soon as he meets her. The young woman captivates him with her beauty, culture and sophistication. But the beginning of WWI nips their romance in the bud. Mikael is sent to a labor camp, from which he manages to escape.

In one of the most harrowing scenes of the film, Mikael rides on top of a cattle train, hoping to elude the Turkish army and make it back to his native village to help his family. Suddenly it starts to rain. He hears strange sounds: terrible moaning and cries. Hands emerge between the grates of the train, trying in vain to cup the drops of water. To his shock, Mikael discovers that hundreds of Armenian civilians are trapped inside, dying of thirst and hunger. Before jumping off the train, the young man manages to pry open the lock to one of the doors and save the trapped prisoners. He finally makes it to his parents' house, where the family has an emotional reunion. However, realizing that it would be too dangerous to stay with his parents, Mikael and his fiancée get married in great haste and move to a remote location, where they live together in a rustic cabin. A few months later, his wife becomes pregnant and experiences health complications.

Meanwhile, his friends, Ana and Chris, visit Mikael's parents trying to locate him. They are helping a group of orphans escape from the murderous Turkish troops. As Mikael joins them on the back roads to lead the orphans to a safer area, he watches helplessly as a group of Turkish soldiers carry off his own family and other inhabitants of his little village, Sirun. He runs to their aid but arrives too late: most of his family and neighbors lie murdered in a ditch. Only his young niece and mother have (barely) survived, left for dead by the Turks. The rest of the beleaguered Armenian community decides that it's better to fight to the death rather than be butchered like sheep by the Turks. Armed with rudimentary tools and a lot of courage, the refugees fight valiantly and manage to hold off the Turkish onslaught until a French ship, le Guichen, comes to their rescue. As Mikael takes a lifeboat of orphans to safety, Ana drowns when her boat is capsized by the Turkish artillery. Despite their rivalry for her love, both Mikael and Chris mourn her death together. This tragedy resolves the tension of the love triangle that had divided them.

The Promise follows in the footsteps of *War and Peace* in depicting war on an epic scale through the optic of a personalized family drama and love story. While viewers seem to rate the film highly, its critical reception has been mixed. *Rotten Tomatoes*, the review aggregator website, reports that, so far, *The Promise* received an average rating of 5.7 out of 10. Benjamin Lee, the film critic for *The Guardian*, found the film "soapy" but well intentioned. Richard Roeper of the *Chicago Sun-Times* concurred, calling it "corny" and "a derivative of better war romances." *The Nation*'s film critic, Pietro A. Shakarian, rated it more highly, claiming, "*The Promise* captures the magnitude of this history (of the Armenian genocide) that no prior film on the genocide has done before."

I agree in part with both perspectives. Like Shakarian, I find *The Promise* to be a moving epic drama that tackles an important and often overlooked subject. At the same time, I feel that the film sometimes privileges the love triangle at the expense of offering viewers more necessary background about the Armenian genocide. For instance, when depicting the friendship between Mikael and Emre (the son of the Turkish official, who is eventually killed because he didn't turn against his Armenian friend), the movie may give viewers the false impression that Turks and Armenians peacefully coexisted before the beginning of the war. But, as I previously indicated, the status of the Armenians living under Ottoman rule was similar to that of the Jews in many European countries: they were considered (at best) second-class citizens and (at worst) enemies to be wiped out in pogroms. In both cases, the sociopolitical conditions were ripe for mass extermination. World Wars were a catalyst for rather than the cause of genocide.

Introduction

Nearly eighty years have passed since the Holocaust. There have been thousands of memoirs, histories and novels written about it, yet many fear that this important event may fall into oblivion. As Holocaust survivors pass away, their legacy of suffering, tenacity and courage could be eventually forgotten. We cannot take Holocaust memories for granted. It is up to each generation to commemorate the victims, preserve their life stories and help prevent such catastrophes. These were my main motivations in writing this book, *Holocaust Memories: A Survey of Holocaust Memoirs, Histories, Novels, and Films* that, as its title suggests, includes over sixty reviews of memoirs, histories, biographies, novels and films about the Holocaust.

It was difficult to choose among the multitude of books on the subject that deserve our attention. I made my selections based partly on the works that are considered to be the most important on the subject; partly on wishing to offer some historical background about the Holocaust in different countries and regions that were occupied by or allied themselves with Nazi Germany, and partly on my personal preferences, interests and knowledge. Because many of the memoirs share geographical and historical contexts, there is some overlap in the background information offered in these reviews. I have tried, however, to keep repetition to a minimum and highlight the unique and valuable contribution of each narrative.

This book offers a general audience, and particularly high school and college students, insight and information into the suffering of nearly six million Jews as well as millions of Gypsies, Poles, Russians and other groups that were considered to be "subhuman" and oppressed by the Nazis. I present the works of others—victims, historians, biographers, fiction writers, and cinematographers—to incite readers to return to these invaluable sources. Furthermore, in order to provide more background into the suffering of the victims, I also offer information about the victimizers: particularly the rulers, politicians, propagandists, military leaders, and "ordinary men," to use Christopher Browning's phrase, who perpetrated the Holocaust. This is why *Holocaust Memories* includes reviews not only of Holocaust memoirs, but also of books that focus on Fascist regimes and their leaders in various countries that enacted genocide or other crimes against humanity.

This book is organized in terms of four main topics: part one consists of the introduction and theoretical framework (Hannah Arendt and totalitarianism); the second part offers an analysis of the perpetrators and Jewish victims of the Holocaust in different countries in Europe; the third presents other victims of the Holocaust (the Poles, the Gypsies, Russian prisoners of war), and the fourth section covers other genocides (in the Soviet Union, China, Cambodia, Rwanda, and North Korea).

Raul Hilberg's monumental studies of the Holocaust, *The Destruction of the European Jews* (New York: Holmes & Meier Publishers, 1985) and *Perpetrators, Victims, Bystanders: The Jewish Catastrophe 1933–1945* (HarperCollins Publishers, 1992), inform many of my reviews, not only in content but also in approach. The historian Robert Jay Lifton rightly calls Hilberg "one of the great scholars of our century. Perhaps more than anyone else, he has exposed the behavior and thought processes of ordinary people carrying out a genocidal project" (front cover of *Perpetrators, Victims, Bystanders*). Although my book does not offer a history of the Holocaust per se, I review numerous history books that deal with the victims, perpetrators, and bystanders of this catastrophe. The works of historians such as Raul Hilberg, Christopher Browning, Max Hastings, Anthony Beevor, Alan Bullock, Robert Conquest, Timothy Snyder, and Robert Jay Lifton inform the background I offer in my discussions of Holocaust memoirs, histories, novels, and films. In these reviews, I present a wide range of narratives about the Holocaust in all of what Hilberg calls its "stages of operation," starting with the racial definition of what constitutes a "Jew"; to the Jews' exclusion from society and the expropriation of their money and property; to their concentration in certain areas and eventually in Jewish Ghettos; to the exploitation of their (slave) labor; and, ultimately, to their annihilation through mass shootings, starvation, medical experimentation, and death camps. (See *The Destruction of the European Jews*, 267.)

Since the Nazis targeted European Jews as their main victims, my book focuses primarily on them. At the same time, since the Nazis also targeted other groups they considered dangerous and inferior, I also review narratives about the sufferings of the Gypsies, the Poles, and other groups that fell victim to the Nazi regimes. As Hilberg aptly puts it, "The Nazi destruction process was, in short, not aimed at institutions; it was targeted at people. The Jews were only the first victims of the German bureaucracy; they were only the first caught in its path" (*The Destruction of the European Jews*, 268). Had

Germany won the war, there's no telling how many more millions would have fallen victim to their race wars. The signs that the Poles and the Slavs would have been the Nazis' next targets for extermination were apparent long before the end of WWII.

In the last section, I review books and films that discuss other genocides and crimes against humanity, including the Stalinist mass purges, the Cambodian massacres by the Pol Pot regime, and the Rwandan genocide. In so doing, I emphasize that history can, indeed, repeat itself, even if in different forms and contexts. Just as the Jews of Europe were not the only targets of genocide, Fascist regimes were not its only perpetrators. If there's one common thread among such diverse human catastrophes its totalitarian institutions. This is why *Holocaust Memories* also includes an analysis of Hannah Arendt's groundbreaking *The Origins of Totalitarianism*. The ethos of mass murder is often initiated from above by authoritarian regimes and disseminated to ordinary citizens through propaganda, indoctrination and terror. The spread of Fascism and Communism during the twentieth century, culminating in the Great Terror and the Holocaust, offers a stark warning to posterity. For as long as we will allow totalitarian regimes and their evil leaders to take root in our societies, we will continue to remain vulnerable to the unspeakable destruction they can cause.

Although I'm writing a book called *Holocaust Memories*, I was born generations later and have no personal memories of the Holocaust. I have vivid childhood recollections of totalitarianism, however, under the Communist regime of Nicolae Ceausescu in Romania: snippets of my family's past and the struggles endured mostly by my parents, which I revisited and wrote about in my first historical novel, *Velvet Totalitarianism* (Rowman & Littlefield Publishing, 2009). In this book, I'm going two generations back in time, to the painful memories of the Holocaust that my grandparents only alluded to. It's mostly their silence that speaks to me now, decades later. I never found out all the details of what happened to my paternal grandfather during the Holocaust in Romania: when and where he was thrown off a train when sent to a forced labor camp by the Antonescu regime during the 1940s, as so many young Jewish men were at the time. All I know is that he survived that fall but walked with a limp for the rest of his life.

My grandparents' survival of the Holocaust in Romania intrigued me enough to start reading scores of books on this subject. I wondered: How could hundreds of thousands of Jews manage to survive in a country that was so virulently anti-Semitic at the time? I learned about Ion Antonescu, the Romanian authoritarian ruler, and his changing and opportunistic policies, which created the apparent paradox of a large number of Jews surviving a pro-Nazi regime that despised them. I also learned about the heroic actions of the Jewish leader Wilhelm Filderman, who never stopped trying to negotiate with Antonescu a livable situation for Romania's Jews. From there, I became interested in exploring deeper what happened to the rest of the European Jews during the Holocaust, nearly six million of whom were obliterated from the face of the Earth and never got the chance to share their tragic stories. This book is dedicated to them, to the survivors who lived with traumatic memories that continued to haunt them, and to the new generations of readers who want to learn about history's darkest past.

Chapter One

Between Fanaticism and Terror

Hitler, Stalin, and The Noise of Time

During WWII, much of Europe was caught in a vice between fanaticism and terror—between Hitler and Stalin. The plight of tens of millions of people falling victim to Stalinism on the one hand and Fascism on the other is eloquently captured by Gustaw Herling, a Polish prisoner in the Soviet Union: "I think with horror and shame of a Europe divided into two parts by the line of the Bug, on one side of which millions of Soviet slaves prayed for liberation by the armies of Hitler, and on the other millions of victims of German concentration camps awaited deliverance by the Red Army as their last hope" (*A World Apart*, 175–76). The similarities between these two evil dictators obsessed with acquiring unlimited power are far greater than their differences. Yet it's worth noting that the two tyrants selected their targets differently. Stalin's purges covered every segment of Soviet society, almost indiscriminately—the Communist party, the Politburo, and the army, navy, and air force—during a period of time when preparations for war should have been a priority.

Julian Barnes, winner of the Man Booker Prize in 2011, describes the arbitrary nature of Stalin's Great Terror in his biographical novel about the composer Dimitri Shostakovich, *The Noise of Time* (New York and London: Knopf, 2016). Tellingly, the title phrase is borrowed from Osip Mandelstam's memoirs, who himself died in a transit camp during the Great Terror of 1938. In personalizing the plight of millions by focusing on the tribulations of a single life—particularly that of a famous musician—Barnes illustrates that nobody was immune to Stalin's subjugating power. Even the great Soviet General and Chief of Staff Mikhail Tukhachevsky, the composer's patron, fell victim to Stalin's paranoia during the purge of the military in June 1937.

By some miracle or good fortune, Shostakovich's life is spared by Stalin. But the composer's reputation isn't, rising and falling with the vicissitudes of the Soviet regime, which the narrator calls "the Power." In 1936, Shostakovich suffers a humiliating reprimand for his opera *Lady Macbeth of the Mtsensk District*, deemed by *Pravda*, the official Soviet newspaper and propaganda mouthpiece, to be representative of the "fidgety, neurotic music" of the bourgeoisie. Although later Stalin personally calls the composer on the phone and undoes some of the damage to his reputation, Shostakovich, along with millions of Soviet citizens, lives in constant fear of the dictator's arbitrary—and often fatal—displays of power.

Success and failure have a way of boiling down to the same thing in totalitarian regimes, which subsume artistic merit to ideological whims and injunctions. Even after Stalin's death, during Nikita Khrushchev's milder authoritarian regime, when the composer is pressured to join the Communist Party in order to become the Chairman of the Russian Federation Union of Composers, Shostakovich feels almost as humiliated and harangued as he did when he was vilified by Stalin's acolytes in *Pravda*. In channeling the character of Shostakovich so compellingly and revealing with a keen sense of irony the arbitrary nature of Soviet totalitarianism, Barnes depicts its inner workings as well as those who had suffered its effects first-hand: authors such as Aleksandr Solzhenitsyn and Eugenia Ginzburg.

By way of contrast to Stalin's arbitrary purges, Hitler honed in on one main target: the Jews. His single-minded focus on destroying the Jewish people could only be called, in his own words, "fanaticism." He remarked: "Any violence which does not spring from a firm spiritual base will be wavering and uncertain. It lacks the stability which can only rest in a *fanatical* outlook" (*Mein Kampf*, 171). There are many hypotheses concerning what might have caused Hitler's hatred of the Jews, ranging from psychological to sociological and biographical explanations. These speculations, however, only make sense in hindsight. Nothing in Hitler's adolescence, when pathology usually shows up, gave any obvious signs of the tremendous anti-Semitic hatred that would later dominate his life.

Biographers state that Hitler was a mediocre student, receiving poor grades in physics, mathematics and German. He performed better in art, but wasn't original. As a young man, he pursued his floundering artistic career in Vienna for about six years. Some state that Hitler's anti-Semitism grew out of his frustration with being rejected by the prestigious Vienna Art Academy. They surmise that he blamed his failure on the Jews. While there may be some truth in this conjecture, there's evidence to the contrary as well. Hitler continued to sell his art and make a living from its sales, supplemented by funds from his family. Interestingly, as Raul Hilberg points out, "Apparently, two of the [art] dealers were Jews" (*Perpetrators, Victims, Bystanders*, 4).

WWI seems to have been a major turning point in Hitler's life. But even then nobody could have guessed that this mediocre soldier would rise to absolute power and wield death and destruction throughout Europe. Hitler was decorated the Iron Cross First Class during the war, but only the second or third time that he was recommended for it: incidentally, by a Jew (Lieutenant Gutmann). At the end of WWI, Hitler was gassed and spent a considerable period of time recuperating in a military hospital. There he had time to contemplate what might have brought about the humiliating defeat of Germany in WWI. After the war, Hitler took a course in Pan-Germanism and became more radicalized in his anti-Semitism. Adolf Gemlich, a German army soldier wrote Hitler a letter asking him about the importance of the "Jewish Question." Hitler wrote Gemlich a response that prefigured the major themes of *Mein Kampf*, his autobiographical treatise written in prison and published in 1925–1926. He distinguished between an anti-Semitism based on reason, or what he called a "rational" and "scientific" anti-Semitism, which would have staying power, and an anti-Semitism based on emotion, manifested by pogroms. Only the former, he stipulated, could efface the Jews from the face of the Earth.

This letter, and particularly the delineation of a systematic and "scientific" anti-Semitism, earned Hitler a reputation on the "Jewish Question" among anti-Semitic radicals opposed to the Weimar Republic. So to return to our earlier question: why did Hitler target the Jews as the main scapegoat and object of his vitriol? He offers a direct answer to this question in *Mein Kampf*:

> The art of leadership as displayed by really great popular leaders in all ages, consists in consolidating the attention of the people against a single adversary.... Where there are various enemies ... it will be necessary to block them all together as forming one solid front, so that the mass of followers in a popular movement may see only one common enemy against whom they have to fight. Such uniformity intensifies their belief in their own cause and strengthens their feeling of hostility towards the opponent. (*Mein Kampf*, 110)

This statement reflects the cold and calculated reasoning Hitler alluded to as early as the note of 1919. He targeted the Jews as his scapegoats and victims for strategic reasons. Hitler's explicit intent was to simplify the root of Germany's social and economic problems to the Jews—considered outsiders in most European countries—and coalesce all forces and people against this common enemy. His choice wasn't primarily a matter of genuine emotion, nor only of pathological hatred. As for Stalin during the Great Terror, it was primarily the product of an insatiable and malicious will to power. This answer—which boils down to power for its own sake—could have never offered a satisfactory response to the question scribbled by victims on cell walls, in prisons, concentration camps and gulags; a question which still echoes to this day: "Zachto—Why?"

Chapter Two

Elie Wiesel's Night

Shedding Light upon the Darkness

Elie Wiesel's memoir *Night* (New York, Hill and Wang, 2006, translated by Marion Wiesel) is one of the best-known and most highly acclaimed works about the Holocaust. The *New York Times* called the 2006 edition "a slim volume of terrifying power." Yet its power wasn't immediately appreciated. In fact, the book may have never been written had Wiesel not approached his friend, the novelist Francois Mauriac, for an introduction to the French Prime Minister Pierre Mendes France, whom he wanted to interview. When Mauriac, a devout Catholic, mentioned that Mendes stated that France was suffering like Jesus, Elie Wiesel responded that ten years earlier he had seen hundreds of Jewish children suffer more than Jesus did on the cross yet nobody spoke about it. Mauriac appeared moved and suggested that Wiesel himself write about this difficult subject.

The young man followed his advice. He began writing in Yiddish an 862-page manuscript about his experiences of the Holocaust. The *Central Union of Polish Jews in Argentina* published an abbreviated version of his book, under the title *And the World Remained Silent*. Wiesel later translated the text into French. He called it, more simply and symbolically, *Night* (*La Nuit*) and sent it to Mauriac, who helped Wiesel find a publisher (the small and prestigious publishing house *Les Editions de Minuit*) and wrote its preface. The English version, published in 1960 by Arthur Wang of *Hill and Wang*, received strong critical acclaim despite initially modest sales. Over the years, Elie Wiesel's eloquent books and informative interviews helped bring the difficult subject of the Holocaust to the center of public attention. In 2006, Oprah Winfrey selected *Night* for her high-profile book club, increasing its public exposure.

This work is autobiographical—an eloquent memoir documenting Wiesel's family sufferings during the Holocaust—yet, due to its literary qualities, the text has also been read as a novel or fictionalized autobiography. The brevity, poignant dialogue, lyrical descriptions of human degradation and suffering, and historical accuracy of this multifaceted work render *Night* one of the most powerful Holocaust narratives ever written.

Elie (Eliezer) Wiesel was only fifteen years old when the Nazis entered Sighet in March of 1944, a Romanian town in Northern Transylvania that had been annexed to Hungary in 1940. At the directives of Adolf Eichmann, who took it upon himself to "cleanse" Hungary of its Jews, the situation deteriorated very quickly for the Jewish population of Sighet and other provincial towns. Within a few months, between May and July 1944, approximately 440,000 Hungarian Jews, mostly those living outside of Budapest, were deported to Auschwitz aboard 147 trains.

Wiesel's entire family—his father Shlomo, mother Sarah, and sisters Tzipora, Hilda, and Beatrice—suffered this fate. Among them, only Elie and two of his sisters, Hilda and Beatrice, survived the Holocaust. However, since women and men were separated at Auschwitz upon arrival, Elie lost track of what happened to his sisters until they reunited after the end of the war. In the concentration camp, father and son clung to each other as the only family they had left.

Night recounts their horrific experiences, which included starvation, forced labor, and a death march to Buchenwald. Being older and weaker, Shlomo becomes the target of punishment and humiliation. He's abused by SS officers as well as by other prisoners who steal his food. Weakened by hunger and fatigue, he dies after a savage beating in January 1945, only a few weeks before the Americans liberate the concentration camp. Throughout their tribulations, the son oscillates between a filial sense of responsibility towards his increasingly debilitated father and regarding his father as a burden that might cost him his own life. Elie doesn't dare intervene when the SS officer beats Shlomo, fearing that he himself would become the next victim if he tries to help his father.

In the darkness and despair of *Night*, the instinct of self-preservation from day to day and moment to moment counteracts a lifetime of familial love. Even when Elie discovers the death of his father in the morning, he experiences a sense of hollowness: not only his father's absence, as his bunk is now occupied by another inmate, but also the lack of his own human response: "I did not weep, and it pained me that I could not weep. But I was out of tears. And deep inside me, if I could have searched the recesses of my feeble conscience, I might have found something like: Free at last" (112).

Night offers a stark psychological account of the process of human degradation in inhumane conditions. Even the relatively few and fortunate survivors of the Nazi atrocities, such as Elie Wiesel, became doubly victimized.

They are the victims of what they suffered at the hands of their oppressors as well as the victims of what they witnessed others suffer and were unable (or unwilling) to help. Although *Night* focuses on the loss of human dignity in the Nazi concentration camps, the author's life would become a quest for regaining it by writing and talking about the Holocaust. As Wiesel explains to his audience on December 10, 1986 during his acceptance speech of the *Nobel Prize* in Oslo, his message to his son—and to the world at large—is about the empathy required to perpetuate Holocaust memories. He declares, "I have tried to keep memory alive, that I have tried to fight those who would forget. Because if we forget, we are guilty, we are accomplices. . . . We must take sides. Neutrality helps the oppressor, never the victim. Silence encourages the tormentor, never the tormented" (118).

Chapter Three

Bergen-Belsen and Four Perfect Pebbles

In a child's imagination, there's a fine line between hope and superstition. For Marion Blumenthal, a nine-year-old Jewish girl imprisoned with her family in the concentration camp Bergen-Belsen, hope means psychological survival in dire conditions, in which death is a near certainty. Holding four pebbles in her hand, the young girl tells her older brother, Albert: "Look closely. I have these three pebbles, exactly matching. Today I will find the fourth. I suppose you think I'm silly" (*Four Perfect Pebbles* co-written by Lila Perl and Marion Blumenthal Lazan, New York: Scholastic, 1996, 7). Although Albert humors his emotional and imaginative sister, for Marion finding the fourth pebble represents the survival of each of her family members: her mother, her father, herself, and her brother.

The memoir *Four Perfect Pebbles* tells the story of the Blumenthal family's survival against all odds. Of German Jewish origin, the Blumenthals flee the anti-Semitic measures adopted by the Nazis in Germany. They believe that they have escaped to relative safety in Holland. As the Nazi empire expands to Holland, however, in 1944 they arrange to be part of a group immigrating to Palestine (in exchange for the release of German POWs). However, to their misfortune, their ship is delayed for three months. Instead of finding their way to Israel, the Blumenthals are sent off first to the Dutch transit camp of Westerbork and later to the "Family Camp" in Bergen-Belsen.

Four Perfect Pebbles offers invaluable historical information about the Holocaust, targeting a young adult audience. The book describes an exceptional story of survival in what became, during the final months of the war, one of the most lethal Nazi camps—the same one, in fact, where the sisters Frank perished. Initially intended as a prisoner of war camp, in 1943 Bergen-

Belsen became a full-fledged concentration camp. Located in Northern Germany, it operated between 1940 and 1945. In June 1943, Bergen-Belsen was designated as a "holding camp" for Jews who were supposed to be exchanged for German prisoners in other countries. Initially, the conditions were relatively good, but with overcrowding they deteriorated. The SS divided the camp into several sections, including the "Hungarian camp," the "Special camp" for Polish Jews, and the "Star camp" for Dutch Jews, where Marion Blumenthal and her family were interned.

Aside from being deprived of sufficient food, water, adequate medical treatment, and basic hygiene facilities, the inmates of Bergen-Belsen were forced to work all day long. Approximately 50,000 people perished there. Bergen-Belsen imprisoned Jews, Poles, Russians, Dutch, Czech, German, and Austrian inmates. In August 1944, the Nazis created a new section, the "Women's Camp," which held about 9,000 women and girls at any given time. In general, the concentration camp became dangerously overcrowded. Over 80,000 people were brought there in cattle trains from camps in Poland and other areas overtaken by the Soviet army.

Unlike Auschwitz, Bergen-Belsen had no gas chambers. Yet as death surrounded her and dozens of corpses were laid out on top of one another outside her barracks each day, Marion lived in constant fear of extermination: "Even though we had been told that there were no gas chambers at Bergen-Belsen, how could we ever be sure? . . . The soap that the prisoners at Bergen-Belsen were given before entering the showers did not guarantee their harmlessness. For it was common practice at Auschwitz to provide victims some soap—and also promise them hot coffee or warm soup afterward—in order to maintain calm and to deceive those about to be gassed" (66–67).

Conditions at Bergen-Belsen deteriorated rapidly towards the end of the war, even by Nazi concentration camp standards. As Marion Blumenthal recalls, "By early 1945 the food at Bergen-Belsen consisted mainly of cabbage-flavored water and moldy bread. This ration was far less than the six hundred calories a day per inmate that the camp had formerly provided. . . . The death toll was now mounting rapidly as the result of exposure, hunger, severe diarrhea, and fevers" (70). Anne and Marion Frank perished there from typhus in February 1945, only weeks before the camp's liberation by the Allies.

When the British and Canadians entered the camp on April 15, 1945, they found thousands of corpses and 60,000 prisoners. Fortunately, Marion and her family were not among them. After having been starved, forced into slave labor, infested by fleas and ill with typhus, the Nazis transported them in cattle trains away from the approaching Soviet army. They were nevertheless found and freed by the Soviets, ending up in a refugee camp in Tröbitz. As she had grasped the four perfect pebbles, Marion continued to hold on to the hope of her family's survival. Unfortunately, her father didn't make it. He succumbed to typhus in May 1945. His death came as a blow to their tight-knit nuclear family. As Marion wistfully notes, "We had come so far, through flight, imprisonment, evacuation, the Nazis' final attempt to destroy us, liberation at last, and now this—freedom and sorrow" (99). Her memoir, *Four Perfect Pebbles*, keeps his memory—and that of countless other Holocaust victims—alive. This book offers a moving testimony of the paradoxical "freedom and sorrow" of being liberated after having suffered so much trauma and the inconsolable loss of loved ones who perished in the Holocaust.

Chapter Four

The Last Seven Months of Anne Frank by Willy Lindwer

The Diary of Anne Frank constitutes one of the most important legacies of the Holocaust. The journal documents the experiences of a young Jewish girl, her family and acquaintances while they hid for years in concealed rooms behind a bookcase, called "the Secret Annex," in Nazi occupied Netherlands. Anne Frank's father, mother and sister moved into the Secret Annex in July 1942. Shortly thereafter they were joined there by the Van Pels family and Fritz Pfeffer, a dentist. Their non-Jewish friends and employees, Victor Kugler, Johannes Keliman, Miep Gies, and Bep Voskuijl, provided them with food supplies as well as with invaluable information about current events, risking the death penalty for harboring and aiding Jews.

In her journal, Anne documents the daily difficulties of living in hiding as well as the family dynamics and challenges of becoming an adolescent in such difficult and dangerous circumstances. However, we know much less about what happened to Anne and her family once the Dutch Nazis caught them. On August 4, 1944, the Secret Annex was stormed by the Grune Polizei, led by the SS officer Karl Silberbauer. The Jewish families were interrogated, then imprisoned in Weteringschans and sent to the punishment barracks for having "illicitly" hid from the Nazis. A few days later, the Frank family and their friends were transferred to Westerbork, a transit camp for Dutch and German Jewish prisoners. On September 3, 1944, they were deported to Auschwitz. The train journey to the concentration camp took three days. There the Franks encountered Anne and Margot's friend from the Jewish Lyceum, Bloeme Evers-Emden. Bloeme was later interviewed about the Frank family by a Dutch filmmaker, Willy Lindwer, for a documentary that would later be published as a book, *The Last Seven Months of Anne Frank* (Doubleday Publishing, New York, 1988).

This book contains several interviews of eyewitnesses and friends who encountered the Frank family at Auschwitz. According to their testimonials, after the men were separated, upon arrival, from the women, Edith Frank and her daughters, Anne and Margot, were sent to Barrack 29. The Frank sisters spent almost two months at Auschwitz in the hospital after they contracted scabies. Their mother stayed there as well to take care of them until Anne and Margot were sent to Bergen-Belsen, probably on October 28, 1944. They were part of a large group of Jewish prisoners who were led on death marches to various concentration camps throughout Germany, as the Russians reoccupied Poland and approached Auschwitz. Within a few months, in January, their mother, Edith Frank, died from sorrow, malnutrition, and exhaustion. Their father, Otto Frank, survived the Holocaust and devoted the rest of his life to preserving his family's legacy—as well as the memory of the Holocaust—by disseminating Anne's diary worldwide.

Although Bergen-Belsen was originally an exchange camp that had better conditions than the concentration and death camps, as previously mentioned, by 1945 it became dangerously overcrowded and disease-ridden as the Germans packed countless prisoners into it. Between July 1943 and the end of 1944, over 9,000 Jews were imprisoned there from countries all over Europe. As more and more Jews were channeled into Bergen-Belsen from other, evacuated labor and concentration camps, by March 1945, the now heavily overcrowded camp reached around 41,000 inmates. The camp was initially run by Commander Adolf Haas, then by Siegfried Seidke and, in its final days, by the sadistic Commander Josef Kramer.

Lindwer states that the conditions became so bad in Bergen-Belsen during the last months of the war that "although there were no gas chambers, ten thousand people died. . . . There was almost nothing to eat, it was winter, and sickness and disease were everywhere. . . . As a result, in the last months before the liberation of Bergen-Belsen and in the first weeks thereafter, most of the inmates perished. Among them were Margot and Anne Frank, who died of typhus within days of each other. The camp was liberated by the British shortly thereafter, on April 15, 1945" (6–7). We still don't know for sure when the Frank sisters passed away. Although Lindwer's book states that they died in March 1945, the Anne Frank Foundation indicates that it probably happened in February.

In a genocide in which millions of people were shot and buried in mass graves or incinerated anonymously in crematoria, Anne Frank's diary, as well as books like Lindwer's, continue to remind us that each life was important and that each death in the Holocaust is worth commemorating.

Chapter Five

Hazy Hints of Memory

After the Holocaust the Bells Still Ring

Early childhood development specialists emphasize the importance of having a nurturing and stable environment for infants and toddlers. That's when the foundations of a child's personality are formed and influence the rest of their life. For instance, studies have shown that many of the children who grew up in the Communist Romanian orphanages during the 1980s—living in deplorable conditions and deprived of love, attention, adequate sanitary facilities, and healthy food—developed personality deficiencies. Many felt emotionally detached from others and could barely communicate.

What about the youngest children of the Holocaust, growing up in the most hellish circumstances imaginable? We know that most of them perished in the fires of the crematoria, being the first to be selected for immediate death. The few so-called lucky child survivors recall bits and pieces of what might have been an even worse fate. Rabbi Joseph Polak's memoir, *After the Holocaust the Bells Still Ring* (New York, Urim Publications, 2015), winner of the 2015 *National Jewish Book Award*, depicts surviving as a toddler in environments whose only certainties were suffering, squalor, misery and death.

Joseph Polak was born on October 16, 1942, in a Jewish family in German-occupied Netherlands. The Dutch Nazis were ready to snatch him from normal life and send his entire family to the transit camp Westerbork before he was even born. His mother recalled the loud pounding on the door in the middle of the night by "the Police" when she was nine months pregnant with Joseph. She courageously warded off the Dutch Nazis by pointing out the advanced state of her pregnancy. Unfortunately, they didn't stay away for long. A year later, on September 29, 1943, the Nazis returned. The Polak family was sent to Westerbork for about four months, joining 100,000 other Jews who would be deported to "the East."

Being so young, Joseph retained only hazy traces of memory of the transit camp, enhanced by his mother's subsequent descriptions: its crowded, sweaty, uncomfortable conditions and the state of anxiety of so many uprooted, displaced people deprived of their roots, assets, professions, families, and identities while awaiting to be sent to what they rightly suspected would be a miserable place. The Dutch government set up Camp Westerbork in the fall of 1939 for Jewish refugees who were not Dutch citizens and had entered the country illegally. Following the German invasion of the Netherlands in 1940, the camp grew and became, between 1942 to 1944, a transit camp for all Dutch Jews on their way to the Nazi concentration camps. While the camp organizers, who were also Jewish, attempted to create some semblance of normalcy through various routines and activities—which included entertaining diversions such as plays and musical shows—inmates were obsessed with the weekly lists of candidates for deportation to the East. Staying versus leaving Westerbork could mean the difference between life and death. Eventually almost everyone was deported.

Joseph and his parents were sent to Bergen-Belsen on February 1, 1944, when the camp was known for its relatively good conditions. Those didn't last long, however. In December 1944, the camp began receiving a large intake of prisoners from Eastern camps evacuated by the Germans faced with the advance of the Soviet army. Grossly overcrowded and without sufficient food and medical supplies or sanitation facilities for its growing population, during its last few months, Bergen-Belsen became a breeding ground for typhus, dysentery, typhoid fever, tuberculosis, and death. Starving and deprived of adequate care, with a mother who had become a shadow of her former self and weighed only 50 pounds, little Joseph wandered around hungry and in rags, playing among the miles of corpses lined up at Bergen-Belsen. The narrator depicts, vividly, the overpowering stench of feces and decomposing bodies. Ultimately, his family was "lucky" again. On April 9, 1945, they were sent along with 2,500 other Jews to Theresienstadt. On the way, they were liberated by the Soviet Army in Tröbitz, a little village of 700 people in East Germany. Unfortunately, by then his parents had lost their health and stamina. His father passed away in May, while his mother fell gravely ill. Joseph was taken by the Dutch authorities and placed in the care of another Dutch-Jewish family.

Joseph doesn't have many memories of this brief period. He only recalls the fleeting impression of security offered by his adoptive father. The young boy held on tightly to the man's jacket as they rode together on a scooter, enjoying the sights and the breeze. Their destination, however, would be a new shock for little Joseph: a white hospital bed where he's reunited with a mother that he can no longer bond with or even recognize. It takes time for mother and child to begin to heal and grow together again in the more livable conditions offered by a center for Jewish survivors in The Hague. They spend there the next three years, from 1945 to 1948. Later, his mother tells Joseph how she managed to put the atrocious conditions of the concentration camp momentarily out of her mind by imagining that she was at her favorite department store, far removed from the squalor of Bergen-Belsen. Then she takes him to that store again. Flashes of memory spark in the child's mind, as he perceives, with a sense of wonder and incomprehensible nostalgia for the sordid yet familiar past, the contrast between the luxurious goods in front of his eyes and the misery of his first years of life. In December 1948, mother and child sail to New York together. Later, they end up living with her family in Montreal.

It took Rabbi Joseph Polak decades to return to his early childhood past, which he only vaguely recalls in bits and pieces, and which, for a long time, he wanted to forget. When he was fifty years old, ten years after his mother had passed away, he returned to Bergen-Belsen after a trip to Paris, where he lectured on Jewish law. He was ready, by then, not only to recollect his family's experiences of the Holocaust, but also to preserve and share them with others. It occurred to him that, as even the youngest child survivors of the Holocaust age and pass away, there is a risk that their memories will disappear along with them. Reading *After the Holocaust the Bells Still Ring* accomplishes more than remind readers of the Holocaust. It also helps us empathize with the victims by placing readers in those circumstances through different narrative means.

Above all, *After the Holocaust the Bells Still Ring* is a beautifully written, evocative memoir. In parts, it's also a theosophical dialogue, staging discussions between the narrator and the Angel of Death on the timeless question of theodicy—namely, how can an omnipotent and omniscient God allow the horrific suffering of children, of innocents? I'm not sure that this question is answered in any definitive manner by the text, but readers can find some solace in the evolution of the author's own life. Rabbi Joseph Polak used his good fortune of being one of the few very young child Holocaust survivors to fill the void of nihilism left by the trauma of his past and make something worthwhile and redeeming of his life. Instead of turning his back upon humanity for what so many did to their fellow human beings, he reached out to help and heal others, both as a religious figure and as a writer.

His narrative is also an educational text. It makes pedagogical bridges with new generations of readers. Where relevant, Rabbi Polak offers helpful historical background and places the Dutch Holocaust in proper perspective. Middle school and high school students, exposed to Anne Frank's diary and little else about the Holocaust in the Netherlands, may perceive the Dutch citizens of the era as heroes who risked their lives to hide Jews from the Nazis. While many courageous individuals certainly did, as Polak points out, the Netherlands was at the same time a country that rounded up Jews with remarkable zeal and efficiency. Between the summer of 1942 and the fall of 1944, the Dutch collaborators sent over 100,000 Jews, or 75 percent of the country's Jewish citizens, to concentration camps. Only 5,200 among them survived. The odds were better for those who went into hiding with the aid of the Dutch underground or of their non-Jewish friends. Of the 30,000 Jews who hid from the Nazis, two thirds survived.

Last but not least, *After the Holocaust the Bells Still Ring* has a beautiful, authentic, and lyrical style. At times, it reminded me of Marguerite Duras's writing—vivid yet also vaguely suggestive, drawing out the philosophical implications of sensory descriptions and versatile in the way it reaches out to readers. Memoir, philosophical and religious treatise, oratory, history lesson, and literary text: You will find all this and more in Joseph Polak's *After the Holocaust the Bells Still Ring*.

Chapter Six

Survivors Club

A Family's Legendary Tale

Michael Bornstein's Holocaust survival story is the stuff that legends are made of. A few years ago, Bornstein ran across a photo of footage taken by Soviet troops of the recently liberated child survivors of Auschwitz. The documentary wasn't actually from the day of liberation of the concentration camp. It was filmed as a reenactment a few days later. The children were asked to put on for one last time the striped, threadbare dingy clothes they wore in the concentration camp. Only this time, they wore them on top of the regular clothes they found in the "Canada" warehouse at Auschwitz, where the Nazis deposited the belongings of prisoners upon arrival. To his own surprise, Michael Bornstein, by now a grandfather, recognized himself in that photograph. He is the gaunt four-year-old boy with wispy, short hair standing in the front. It was miraculous that he had survived since the odds were heavily stacked against him.

Out of the millions of inmates at Auschwitz, fewer than 3,000 were liberated by the Soviets and only fifty-two of them were children under the age of eight. Seeing this picture stirred something in Michael—not so much full-fledged memories, since he had been too young to remember the horrors of the Holocaust, as the desire to record his family's incredible survival story. With the help of archival research, his father's documents and interviews with neighbors and surviving relatives, Michael Bornstein and his daughter, NBC, and MSNBC News producer Debbie Bornstein Holinstat, co-wrote his Holocaust memoir, aptly calling it *Survivors Club: The True Story of a Very Young Prisoner of Auschwitz* (Farrar, Straus and Giroux, 2017). Although the title alludes primarily to the handful of children who survived Auschwitz, it also refers to Michael's family. Out of the 3,200 Jews living in Zarki at the time of the Nazi invasion in September 1939, only about thirty survived the war. Most of them were members of the Bornstein family.

Historically, Michael Bornstein's family and their neighbors experienced firsthand almost every stage of the Nazi atrocities in Poland. Upon invading their little town, Zarki, the Wehrmacht burned it to the ground. They rounded up hundreds of Jews and shot them in nearby forests, in the streets and even in their own homes. Soon thereafter, the Nazis set up a Jewish Ghetto. Unlike larger ghettos throughout Poland, however, for most of its existence, the one in Zarki remained open, allowing some life-sustaining trade and interaction with the local Polish population. Michael's father, Israel Bornstein, was elected Jewish Council President, a heavy responsibility that he reluctantly accepted. He and his resilient and courageous wife, Sophie, did their best to protect not only their own nuclear family—their older son Samuel and the younger son Michael, who was still a baby—but also the entire Jewish community of their town.

As in the case of the other Jewish ghettos in Poland, life for Jews in Zarki was a constant struggle to ward off hunger, forced labor and the relentless waves of deportations to death camps. For a while, Israel Bornstein managed to round up the resources to bribe the local Gestapo chief, Officer Schmitt, into giving their community more food and occasionally diminishing their burden. Schmitt, though a callous man and a true Nazi believer, was fortunately also venal. But small-scale bribery proved to be no match for the immense Nazi killing machine. By the end of September 1942, most of the Jewish inhabitants of Zarki were sent to die at Treblinka. Perhaps wishing to demonstrate his "humanity," Schmitt made one exception. He spared Israel Bornstein and his nuclear family from death. They, along with Israel's mother (Dora), were sent to a more lenient labor camp until they, too, were eventually dispatched to Auschwitz. As Michael was to find out later, his father and older brother both perished there.

Michael, by now a toddler, was placed in a children's section of the concentration camp. Had his mother not managed to sneak him into the women's camp after a few weeks, he most likely wouldn't have made it. The older children, themselves starving, were constantly stealing most of his meager portions of daily gruel. Under the wing of his mother and grandmother, Michael managed to live in hiding from day to day. When his mother was reassigned to another labor camp, the little boy was left under the sole protection of his paternal grandmother. Ironically, it was illness that ultimately saved his life. Suffering from a high fever, he was placed in the infirmary around the time the Nazis began to force the Auschwitz prisoners on the fatal death marches. From the infirmary window, Michael watched the beleaguered, freezing prisoners file away from the camp under the blows of the Nazi guards. His liberation by the Allies a few days later is captured by the

Soviet footage. But the inspiring story of his survival—*Survivors Club*—has only now been told.

Chapter Seven

Primo Levi's Reflection on Humanity in Crisis

Survival in Auschwitz

Primo Levi's memoir, *Survival in Auschwitz* (New York: Simon & Schuster, 1996, translated by Giulio Einaudi), depicts not only the author's survival in the notorious Nazi concentration camp, but also the survival of his humanity after enduring such a grueling process of dehumanization. Published in 1947 under the Italian title *If This is a Man (Se questo e un uomo)*, Levi doesn't claim to offer new information about the Holocaust in this autobiographical book. Nor does he wish to level fresh accusations against the Nazis. Writing in an introspective manner, Levi sets out "to furnish documentation for a quiet study of certain aspects of the human mind" (9).

Pensive and thought provoking, *Survival in Auschwitz* constitutes a reflection on the power—and limits—of forgiveness. In an interview published by the *New Republic* on February 16, 1986, Levi announces that he did not harbor any feelings of hatred towards the Germans. He explains: "I regard hatred as bestial and crude, and prefer that my actions and thoughts be the product, as far as possible, of reason. Much less do I accept hatred directed collectively at an ethnic group, for example at all the Germans." Levi views the Holocaust not as a reflection of the German nation, but rather as a broader crisis of humanity. Nation after nation fell under the spell of Fascism as countless individuals engaged in horrific acts of cruelty.

Does this mean that the author absolves the Nazis of moral responsibility for their actions? No. During the same interview, Levi qualifies: "All the same, I would not want my abstaining from explicit judgment to be confused with an indiscriminate pardon." He explains that he can only forgive those who show—through actions, not just words—that they take responsibility and feel guilty for their crimes against humanity. He is speaking, above all, of the crimes perpetrated by ordinary men and women.

In *Survival in Auschwitz* Levi describes how inflicting harm upon others became a matter of routine during the Holocaust. Sometimes, even without harboring any particular hatred, many Nazi officers conducted the selection process and sent hundreds of thousands of people to their deaths in the gas chambers. Two of the main questions that continue to haunt Levi throughout his life are: how mass murder could have become so commonplace and how much did the German population know about the Holocaust.

In his 1986 interview with the *New Republic*, Levi offers lucid and reasonable answers. Because totalitarian regimes function very differently from democracies, he argues, it's not possible to have a dissemination of truthful information and open criticism of despicable actions in totalitarian regimes that we have in democratic societies. Yet, by the same token, Levi remarks, "It was not possible to hide the existence of the enormous concentration camp apparatus from the German people. What's more, that was not (from the Nazi point of view) even desirable. Creating and maintaining an atmosphere of undefined terror in the country was one of the aims of Nazism."

Perhaps one of the most astute observations in *Survival in Auschwitz* is the statement that just as absolute happiness is impossible, so is absolute unhappiness. Even in the hellish conditions of the Nazi concentration camps, prisoners gradually adapt to each phase of the process of dehumanization: starting with the isolation from the rest of the population in Jewish ghettos; to the order to gather by the train station to be transported in cattle trains to concentration camps; to the brutal conditions of the camps themselves. It is rarely a planned acquiescence to humiliation and abuse. Rather, at each phase of their oppression, victims tend to focus on the moment-to-moment struggle for survival. Heroism in such adverse conditions becomes almost impossible. By way of contrast, as Levi observes, "to sink is the easiest of matters; it is enough to carry out all the orders one receives, to eat only the ration, to observe the discipline of the work and the camp" (*Survival in Auschwitz*, 90). In such a context, the quest for survival assumes heroic dimensions itself, as does the ability to endure extreme hardship while remaining dignified and humane. Few are able to achieve this. Among them is Levi's friend, Lorenzo, a man whom the author remembers fondly for the rest of his life.

When asked, in the *New Republic* interview, why a grander, more ambitious heroism didn't occur in the camps—"How is it that there were no large-scale revolts?"—Levi reminds readers that in such closely monitored environments, "Escape was difficult and extremely dangerous. The prisoners were debilitated, besides being demoralized, by hunger and ill treatment. Their heads were shaved, their striped clothing was immediately recognizable, and their wooden clogs made silent and rapid walking impossible."

Furthermore, most of the inmates found themselves imprisoned in foreign countries whose inhabitants spoke a different language. Many of the natives were hostile to Jews and most were indifferent to their plight. As for revolts, as Levi points out, they existed in Treblinka, Sobibor, and Birkenau. However, "They did not have much numerical weight. Like the Warsaw Ghetto uprising, they represented, rather, examples of extraordinary moral force. In every instance they were planned and led by prisoners who were privileged in some way, and consequently in better physical and spiritual condition than the average camp prisoner."

Although, philosophically speaking, Levi remained a humanist and rationalist throughout his life despite the severe trauma he endured at Auschwitz, he eventually succumbed to its effects. Depression and nightmares haunted him throughout his life. In April 1987, Levi died after falling from his third-story apartment in Turin, which many close to him considered a suicide. Yet he did not write, suffer and die in vain. Through his memoirs, books, and interviews, Primo Levi left behind an invaluable intellectual legacy that helps us recall, commemorate, and better comprehend the worst humanitarian crisis in history.

Chapter Eight

Sarah's Key and the Holocaust in France

Between 1940 and 1944, during the German occupation, approximately 75,000 Jews were deported from France. Most of them perished in the Nazi concentration camps. Despite these grim statistics, France was one of the European countries with the highest Jewish survival rate—roughly 75 percent. Out of 340,000 Jews living in the country, about 72,500 died during the Holocaust. Initially, part of France retained some autonomy: the Vichy regime led by Marshal Philippe Petain signed an armistice with Germany. German anti-Semitic measures against the Jewish population of France began almost immediately, including forcing Jews to wear the yellow star and prohibiting them from working in white-collar professions as lawyers, teachers, government officials, and journalists. Observing a similar procedure in France as in the rest of occupied Europe, the Germans created a *Judenrat*, the *Union Generale des Israelites de France*, to better control the Jewish population through a centralized administration.

Harsher repressive measures soon followed. In August 1941, over 4,000 Jews were incarcerated at the Drancy internment camp, to be deported to Auschwitz in March 1942. The French police rounded up 13,000 Jews in Paris—including 4,000 children—during the *Velodrome D'Hiver* roundup of July 1942. They were held there in horrible conditions without heat, water, food, or sanitation facilities. A few committed suicide by throwing themselves off the bleachers. The French municipal police carried the roundups on their own, without help from the SS. Emile Hennequin, the Director of Police in Paris, officially ordered that the arrest of over 13,000 Jews "must be effected with maximum speed, without speaking and without comment." The arrested were not given the opportunity to pack or even say goodbye to their loved ones.

The novel *Sarah's Key* (St. Martin's Griffin, 2008), written by Tatiana de Rosnay and originally published in France under the title *Elle s'appelait Sarah* (*She was named Sarah*), captures this dire period of French history. The novel personalizes the atrocity by narrating the fictionalized story of Sarah Starzynski, a ten-year-old Jewish girl living with her parents and four year old brother in Paris, who are rounded up by the French police in July 1942 and confined in the Velodrome d'Hiver. The little boy is left behind when the police arrive. In the panic of the moment, Sarah hides her brother in a camouflaged closet that blends in with the wall, planning to let him out upon returning a few hours later. She makes him promise her not to get out until she comes back.

However, Sarah and her parents don't get the opportunity to return home. The parents are eventually deported to Auschwitz, where they perish. Sarah manages to escape with another Jewish girl, Rachel, to the countryside where they are hidden by a couple, Jules and Genevieve Dufaure, farmers with a good heart. While Rachel dies of dysentery, Sarah survives and remains obsessed with saving her younger brother. The couple disguises her as a boy and together they take the train back to Paris. By then, as Sarah discovers, her family's apartment has already been reallocated to a non-Jewish French family. Sarah rings the doorbell and, as soon as she's let in, rushes to the hidden closet. When she opens the door, she's horrified to find inside the corpse of her little brother, who unfortunately had kept his promise to wait for her.

This tragic family tale is investigated sixty years later by journalist Julia Jarmond, whose in-laws inhabited the Jewish family's former apartment in Paris. Julia, an American living in Paris, struggles with a troubled marriage with Frenchman Bertrand Tezac, who cheated on her with another woman. When Julia discovers that she's pregnant and decides to keep the baby, Bertrand, who was planning to leave his wife for his mistress, feels trapped. The unhappy couple eventually divorces. Julia finds renewed purpose in raising her baby girl, whom she tellingly names Sarah, and in tracking down the family history that led her to this series of revelations about the Holocaust. *Sarah's Key* may not be historical in the strict sense of the term since, as the author admits, its main characters are fictional. Yet this imaginary journey into the past uncovers one of the darkest—and very real—chapters in French history.

Chapter Nine

The Holocaust in Hungary

Leni Yahil's The Holocaust

Historian Leni Yahil estimates that in 1941 there were approximately 762,000 Jews living in Hungary, about a fourth of whom lived in Budapest (*The Holocaust*, Oxford: Oxford University Press, 1990, 506). Under pressure from Nazi Germany, the conservative regime of Admiral Miklos Horthy and Prime Minister Miklos Kallay instituted anti-Semitic measures modeled after the Nuremberg Laws. However, up to 1944, Horthy didn't agree with the Nazi policy of deporting and exterminating Hungarian Jews. The Communist politician Bela Vago described the Horthy regime as a contradictory mixture of authoritarianism and some openness to democratic input, with anti-Semitic attitudes and relative tolerance toward the native Jewish population in Hungary:

> This was one of the paradoxical phenomena of the Hungarian regime, which contained a mixture of vestiges of feudalism with democratic-parliamentary elements; the authoritarianism of a quasi-fascistic regime with tolerance towards the democratic opposition; an official anti-Semitic policy with tolerance toward Jews in the fields of journalism, the arts, and other areas of culture. The Jews could be active as members of Parliament until the German occupation in 1944. (Cited by Leni Yahil in *The Holocaust*, 507)

Following the Soviet victory in the battle of Stalingrad, Horthy and Kallay began to realize that Germany might lose the war. Kallay sent out feelers to the Allies, hoping to negotiate an armistice with favorable terms for Hungary. When Hitler found out about this strategic move, Germany occupied Hungary. Horthy was allowed to remain the figurehead leader of Hungary, but Kallay was replaced with the fanatical pro-Nazi general Dome Sztojay.

The latter fell into step with the Final Solution program and agreed to deport the Jews.

Adolf Eichmann personally came to Hungary along with a team of "experts," which included Dr. Siefried Seidel (the former Commandant of Theresienstadt), Theodor Dannecker (in charge of the Jewish deportations from France, Bulgaria and Italy) and Dieter Wisliceny (who had been in charge of deporting the Greek and Slovakian Jews). Although Eichmann was ever-present in Hungary, efficiently organizing the deportation of the approximately 450,000 Jews living outside Budapest, he preferred to let the Hungarian gendarmes do the dirty work of rounding up the Jews in ghettos and sending them by cattle trains or via grueling death marches to concentration camps. In allowing for this "local initiative," Eichmann hoped to appease the Hungarian leadership's nationalist sentiments by giving them the illusion of autonomy. As he later boasted, "Over the years, I have learned from experience which hooks I have to use to catch which fish" (*The Holocaust*, Yahil, 505). In less than two months, by August 1944, the Hungarian authorities and the SS sent over 440,000 Jews from the provinces to concentration camps. All that was left in Hungary were the Jews of Budapest.

Given that Germany was losing the war, Admiral Horthy hesitated to deport the Jews of the Hungarian capital. He worried that this act would create a public outcry in the international press and provoke the Western Allies. Although under increased pressure from Eichmann and his team to eliminate the Hungarian Jews, Horthy put a stop to the deportations. He also dismissed Sztojay and began negotiating an armistice with the Soviets. In response, the Germans staged a coup and set up an even more extreme pro-Nazi government, led by Ferenc Szalasi, the leader of the Arrow Cross, whose members were notorious for their barbarism and anti-Semitism. In the process of rounding up the Jews of Budapest into a Ghetto, the Arrow Cross hooligans manifested great cruelty. They looted, beat, raped and murdered hundreds of Jews. Thousands were forced into death marches across the Austrian border while hundreds, including toddlers and children, were pushed into the ice-cold Danube River. All in all, Szalasi's Arrow Cross gendarmes brutally murdered 15,000 Jews.

It is largely due to the heroic efforts of the Swedish diplomat Raoul Wallenberg, which I'll discuss in greater detail in the next chapter, that about 140,000 Jews survived in the Hungarian capital. The Soviets marched into Budapest on January 1945 and drove the Nazis and their Arrow Cross allies out of power by that spring. Unfortunately, when he tried to meet with a Soviet general to help the Jews left in the Budapest ghetto, Wallenberg was taken prisoner by the NKVD. Despite his valiant efforts during the war, only a small percentage of Hungarian Jews lived through the Holocaust. Out of the nearly 800,000 Jews living in Hungary during the early 1940's, less than a third survived.

Chapter Ten

A Holocaust Hero in Hungary

Wallenberg by Kati Marton

The Talmud states, "Whoever destroys a soul, it is as if he destroyed the whole world. And whoever saves a life, it is as if he saved the whole world" (Mishnah Sanhedrin 4:9, *Babylonian Talmud*, Tractate Sanhedrin 37a). Raoul Wallenberg, a Swedish diplomat, followed this tenet. He did everything in his power to save as many Jews as possible in Nazi occupied Hungary.

Wallenberg's own life story contains as much triumph as tragedy. By the time Wallenberg, then only thirty-one years old, arrived in Budapest, 437,000 Hungarian Jews living outside the capital had already been deported to Auschwitz. He could do nothing to save them. But there were approximately 230,000 Jews left in Budapest, all of whom Adolf Eichmann, who was stationed in the capital, planned to send as expediently as possible to their deaths. The preparations of the giant death machine were already underway. Most of the Jews living in Budapest had already been herded by the Nazis and their Fascist (Arrow Cross) collaborators into a Jewish Ghetto. They were deprived of any means of subsistence and living in terror. Every day they were subject to Nazi deportations and at the mercy of mob pogroms incited by the Hungarian Fascist group, the Arrow Cross.

Facing a humanitarian crisis where time was of the essence, Wallenberg proved to be flexible and resourceful. He didn't limit himself to traditional, slow diplomatic measures to save Budapest's Jewish community. Using his own funds, he cajoled and bribed members of the Arrow Cross as well as German officials in Budapest to protect the lives of approximately 100,000 Jews. Responding promptly to calls for help, he issued tens of thousands of official-looking Swedish Embassy protection papers to the desperate Jewish community.

Kati Marton's biography *Wallenberg: The Incredible True Story of the Man Who Saved the Jews of Budapest* (New York: Arcade Publishing, Centenary Edition, 2011) narrates the life of this courageous and altruistic man. It also explores the unsolved mystery surrounding his death while imprisoned in the Soviet Union. Having managed to save tens of thousands of innocent lives and to survive WWII and the Nazi terror in occupied Hungary, in an ironic twist of fate, Wallenberg perished at the hands of the Allies. He was caught in the lethal web of the Soviet Secret Police, the NKVD. Yet he managed to accomplish so much in his short lifetime.

By the time he reached Hungary in his early thirties, Raoul Wallenberg had already lived a full life. Born in an affluent family of Swedish bankers and industrialists, young Raoul preferred to travel and learn about different cultures rather than devoting himself to making money. Although he probably could have selected any university in Europe, he chose to study at the University of Michigan in Ann Arbor, eager to learn more about the United States. He also travelled to Haifa, Palestine. Through family connections he met Koloman Lauer, a Hungarian Jew who was the Director of a Swedish Import and Export Company, the Mid-European Trading Company. Within a few months, the young man impressed Lauer so much with his competence and efficiency that he became a joint partner in this enterprise. Given Lauer's family and business ties to Hungary, Wallenberg traveled to Budapest, following closely the rapidly deteriorating political situation in the country. He was especially touched—and alarmed—by the fate of the Jews.

Wallenberg also took trips to Vichy France and Nazi Germany. He learned about how their bureaucracies and killing machines worked. His observations that the Nazi regime functioned through a mixture of need for respectability and natural authority served him well as he embarked on the dangerous mission of saving Budapest's Jews. He bribed corruptible officials with cigars, alcohol or food—a strategy that proved to be quite effective in a time of severe shortages—while at the same time issuing official-looking passports and protective orders, couched in formal language, under the auspices of the Swedish Embassy and government. At one point, he even confronted the "Engineer of death" himself, Adolf Eichmann, in a showdown of wills from which the Nazi official backed down. Wallenberg managed to save hundreds of Jews right before a cattle train was about to carry them off to Auschwitz.

On January 17, 1945, following the Ally victory and Budapest's encirclement by the Soviet army, Wallenberg and his chauffeur drove, accompanied by a Soviet military escort, to meet with a high-ranking Soviet general. Wallenberg hasn't been heard from since. Marton's book indicates that several eyewitnesses claim they have seen him in the notorious Soviet prison, the Lyubianka, and later in several gulags well into the 1970s. However, such information remains highly speculative. The evidence points to the fact that Wallenberg perished in 1947 at the hands of the NKVD. The heroic man who saved countless lives from the Nazis could not himself be saved from the totalitarian killing machine.

Chapter Eleven

Imre Kertesz's Fatelessness

When Luisa Zielinski interviewed the Hungarian writer Imre Kertesz, 2002 *Nobel Prize in Literature* winner and Holocaust survivor, in the *Paris Review* during the summer of 2013, the author was already suffering from Parkinson's disease (Imre Kertesz, "The Art of Fiction," *Paris Review* No. 220, interviewed by Luisa Zielinksi). Despite being gravely ill, Kertesz spoke with characteristic lucidity about his fiction as well as about the Holocaust. Born in 1929 in Budapest, as a young man Kertesz was deported to Auschwitz in 1944 for a short period of time, and then transferred to Buchenwald. Although his books deal with his experience of the Holocaust, they are not, strictly speaking, autobiographical. Kertesz views his description of the Holocaust in *Fatelessness* (Vintage Editions, 2004) as a rupture of civilization that the entire world should examine and take seriously rather than as an anecdote of his own difficult childhood experiences. "I was interned in Auschwitz for one year," he recalls. "I didn't bring back anything, except for a few jokes, and that filled me with shame. Then again, I didn't know what to do with this fresh experience. For this experience was no literary awakening, no occasion for professional or artistic introspection."

As the author recounts during his *Paris Review* interview, he didn't feel destined to be a writer. Rather, Kertesz became a writer by painstakingly editing his own texts. The process of writing wasn't easy, both because of the difficult subject matter and because he had to hide his endeavors from the Communist regime. In fact, totalitarian repression forms a common thread between his experience of Nazism and Communism. "I was suspended in a world that was forever foreign to me, one I had to reenter each day with no hope of relief. That was true of Stalinist Hungary, but even more so under National Socialism," he declares.

Fatelessness offers an intimate psychological account of a young man's disconcerting experience of being uprooted from his family, schoolmates and friends to be thrust into the alien and brutal world of the Nazi concentration camps. Gyorgy Koves, the fifteen-year-old protagonist, first loses his father, who dies in a Nazi labor camp. His stepmother and a Hungarian employee continue taking care of the family store. They fall in love, survive the war and eventually marry each other. But Gyorgy (George) is rounded up by the Arrow Cross and first sent to forced labor, then deported to Auschwitz. *Fatelessness* depicts his experiences there.

One of the most unique aspects of the narrative is its temporality. The adolescent narrator describes his experiences in the present tense, as if writing a journal. He notes every character's expression and creates realistic dialogues without offering much judgment or analysis. Kertesz considers this observational technique as appropriate for a child narrator. As he explains, "a child has no agency in his own life and is forced to endure it all." While few Jewish victims had much agency during the Holocaust, adults at least had the emotional maturity to realize what was happening to them. Children, on the other hand, were swept up by the Nazi extermination machine without being able to comprehend the events that destroyed their lives or to do anything about them.

Given the almost existentialist nature of Kertesz's writing, how much of *Fatelessness* is based on the author's life and how much of it is historical fiction becomes less relevant than the narrative's powerful and immediate connection to generations of readers interested in learning about the Holocaust. Despite its tone of despair, the book's most powerful message is one of hope: the belief that one can save one's humanity even in the direst historical circumstances.

Chapter Twelve

Anti-Semitism in Hungary Today

Anti-Semitism has a long history in Hungary, nearly as long as the history of the Jews living in the country. Hitler was not the first to prescribe armbands to mark, isolate, and shame the Jews. King Ladislaus IV of Hungary (1272–1290) commanded that each Jewish person should wear a piece of red cloth. During the fourteenth century, Jews were suspected of spreading the plague and expelled en masse from the country. Two centuries later, King Ladislaus II (1490–1516) accused the Jews of ritual murder and burned them at the stake. The Diet of 1686 declared that Jews were not subjects of Hungary because they were not Christian (they were categorized as "unbelievers"). Queen Maria Theresa (1740–1780), perhaps emulating Catherine the Great of Russia (who segregated the Jews into a large area called the Pale of Settlement), expelled the Jews from Buda.

It is only during the modern period, under the reign of the Enlightened monarch Joseph II (1780–1790), that Hungarian Jews attained minority rights. The National Assembly officially emancipated them half a century later, in 1849, which enabled the vast majority of the Jews living in Hungary to integrate well into the country. This was particularly true of the Jews of Budapest, who constituted almost a quarter of the city's population. The Nazi influence upon the authoritarian regime of Miklos Horthy, and the rise to power of the Fascist Arrow Cross movement, undid over a century of civil rights progress. In 1944, the Holocaust nearly wiped out the Jewish population of Hungary, killing 450,000 Jews.

The current Jewish population of Hungary remains very small. About 110,000 Jews live in the country, roughly the same number as right after WWII. Most of them live in Budapest and consider themselves to be assimilated in Hungarian society. In fact, only about 10 percent of Hungarian Jews identify themselves as "Jewish" by religion. Nonetheless, over the past two decades Hungary has experienced a dramatic rise in anti-Semitism. Abraham H. Foxman, the National Director of the Anti-Defamation League, states, "In Hungary, Spain and Poland the numbers for anti-Semitic attitudes are literally off-the-charts and demand a serious response from political, civic and religious leaders." In 2014 the ADL declared Hungary as the most anti-Semitic country in Europe. According to its survey, 50 percent of young Hungarians (under the age of thirty-five) have anti-Semitic attitudes.

Not surprisingly given these statistics, contemporary Hungary has experienced a rise in neo-Nazi and other authoritarian anti-Semitic political parties and groups, such as the HunterSS, White Storm, Endlosung, and the illegal paramilitary group the Hungarian National Front. In May 2014, Apathy Istvan Laszlo, a representative of the right wing nationalist party Jobbik ("The Movement for a Better Hungary"), which aims at the preservation of "Hungarian interests and values" in the city Erzsebetvaros, even went so far as to publically state on his Facebook profile that the historical accounts of the Holocaust were exaggerated. He claimed that "the Jewish background superpower" was responsible for the Holocaust. Contradicting himself, Laszlo has denied that the Holocaust ever happened.

The dramatic rise of anti-Semitism in a country with so few Jews—most of whom identify themselves as assimilated Hungarians—confirms one of the important lessons of the Holocaust: namely, that anti-Semitism is an attitude that has little to do with the object of ethnic hatred. It has a lot to do with authoritarian political parties that predicate their nationalist agenda on a mythical sense of national identity formed by the exclusion and denigration of groups marked as "Other."

Chapter Thirteen

Hannah Arendt's The Origins of Totalitarianism

Why the Jews?

Hailed as a classic by the *Times Literary Supplement* and ranked by *Le Monde* as one of the 100 best books of twentieth century, Hannah Arendt's monumental study, *The Origins of Totalitarianism* (1951), sketches a political philosophy of the rise of Nazism and Stalinism. In the first part of the book, Arendt refutes common misconceptions about anti-Semitism. Her arguments focus upon a central question: How and why did the Jewish people throughout Europe come to be targeted for discrimination, abuse, mass deportation and extermination?

THE RISE IN NATIONALISM DID NOT CAUSE A CORRESPONDING RISE IN ANTI-SEMITISM IN EUROPE

One common answer to this question explains the radical rise of anti-Semitism in Europe in terms of the growth of nationalist sentiments and "xenophobic outbursts." Arendt contends that just the opposite holds true: modern anti-Semitism increased as nationalism declined throughout Europe. Nazi ideology, while making use of nationalist sentiments in its rhetoric, actually emphasized the international character of "race." Hitler never hid the fact that his aim was to ensure the supremacy of the "Aryan" race in Europe and, if possible, throughout the world by subjugating and even eliminating "inferior races." He turned prevalent feelings of nationalist fervor, anti-Semitism and xenophobia into an international racial war.

THE JEWS WERE NOT RANDOMLY SELECTED AS NAZI IDEOLOGY'S MAIN TARGET AND VICTIMS

Arendt goes on to refute another common misconception—namely, that the Nazi movement could have selected any other group as its main target of hatred and abuse. After all, it did include other groups in its categories of "undesirables," such as the mentally handicapped, Gypsies and Poles. Nonetheless, the isolation and extermination of the Jews was Hitler's—and, consequently, the Nazi movement's—primary obsession. The Nazis pursued the mass deportations and extermination of Jews at the cost of economic losses. They persisted even after the battle of Stalingrad, when they began to lose the war. This is not, Arendt qualifies, because the Jews are perpetual scapegoats and victims. "The theory that the Jews are always the scapegoat implies that the scapegoat might have been anyone else as well," she points out. "It upholds the perfect innocence of the victim, an innocence which insinuates not only that no evil was done but that nothing at all was done that might possibly have a connection with the issue at stake" (*The Origins of Totalitarianism*, 5). So then why were the Jews targeted as the Nazi regimes' primary enemies and targets throughout Europe?

THE JEWS WERE TARGETED BY THE NAZIS LARGELY BECAUSE OF THEIR STATELESSNESS AND POWERLESSNESS

Nazi propaganda held the Jews responsible for everything that went wrong: economic crises, Germany's humiliation in the Treaty of Versailles following the country's defeat in WWI, unemployment, etc. It implied that the Jews were a unified people that had vast political power. Hitler described his war against the Jews as a self-defense against the "Jewish conspiracy" to take over the world. Yet, Arendt maintains, the opposite holds true. "Anti-Semitism reached its climax when Jews had similarly lost their public functions and their influence, and were left with nothing but their wealth" (*The Origins of Totalitarianism*, 4). Arendt compellingly argues that Jewish wealth without political power and social influence began to be seen as parasitic. It provoked envy rather than respect and contempt rather than compassion, particularly in those looking for scapegoats to take blame for their economic troubles.

TOTALITARIANISM SUBJUGATES PERFECTLY OBEDIENT PEOPLE

No doubt, there's a personal, quirky and irrational component to Hitler's obsessive hatred of the Jewish people, which became part and parcel of his insatiable thirst for power. Hitler justified his desire for total control not only of the German people, but also of Europe and eventually the world, in terms of "saving" the Aryan race from contamination and eventual destruction by the Jews. Yet he targeted Jewish victims who not only had no desire to take over the world, but also didn't have the means to do so. In general, Arendt argues, the victims of totalitarian terror were selected because of their helplessness and innocence, not because of their power and culpability. The assault upon the Jewish people, she goes on to illustrate, was only the first step in a reign of terror of unprecedented proportions that would aim at nothing short of the destruction of ethical values and of human identity itself.

Chapter Fourteen

The Role of the Masses in The Origins of Totalitarianism

Totalitarianism isn't an easy phenomenon to grasp. It's difficult to understand how hundreds of millions of people throughout Europe and the Soviet Union could have allowed the horrors of the Holocaust and the Stalinist mass purges to take place. In *The Origins of Totalitarianism*, Hannah Arendt offers one of the most cogent explanations for these mass horrors. "Mass" is the key word here. Arendt describes a modern social entity called "the masses," which she distinguishes from the mob (itself capable of spurts of violence, such as during pogroms) as well as from classes (groups based on shared economic circumstances and interests). The masses, she declares, are a totalitarian phenomenon.

MASSES VERSUS CLASSES

Arendt posits that one of the key features of the totalitarian state is its system of indoctrination, propaganda, isolation, intimidation, and brainwashing—instigated and supervised by the Secret Police—which transforms classes, or thoughtful individuals capable of making relatively sound political decisions, into masses, or people who have been so beaten down that they become apathetic and give their unconditional loyalty to the totalitarian regime.

Unlike classes, Arendt explains, masses are amorphous and easily swayed. They're moved by superficial rhetoric and empty fervor rather than united by a common identity or shared economic interests. According to Arendt, "The term masses applies only when we deal with people who either because of their sheer numbers, or indifference, or a combination of both, cannot be integrated into any organization based on common interest" (*The

Origins of Totalitarianism, 311). This political and social apathy isn't enough for people to lend their support to totalitarian movements, however. An additional factor comes into play. The apathetic masses must come under the spell of charismatic malevolent leaders, like Hitler and Stalin, who gain control over society and destroy the last vestige of human decency and individualism. If the masses don't exist in sufficient numbers in a given society, then totalitarian rulers institute policies that create them. This was the main purpose, Arendt contends, of Stalin's relentless purges, which undermined any real class identity and eroded ideological conviction. Even the nuclear family and bonds of love unraveled, as friends distrusted friends and parents lived under the reasonable fear that their own children could at any moment turn them in to the Secret Police for "deviationism" from the party line.

SOCIAL GROUPS VERSUS ATOMIZED INDIVIDUALS

The masses are vast in number but isolated in nature. Totalitarian society creates a conglomeration of atomized individuals. There's no other way to command absolute obedience to the regime: even when the government's policies change radically, demanding one thing of its followers one day and the opposite the next. Unconditional loyalty, Arendt argues, "can be expected only from the completely isolated human being who, without any other ties to family, friends, comrades, or even mere acquaintances, derives his sense of having a place in the world only from his belonging to a movement, his membership in the party" (*The Origins of Totalitarianism*, 323–4). This illusory sense of belonging can't be based on any real social identity, since totalitarian movements are arbitrary in their demands, fickle in their objectives and unstable in their actions. Perhaps their only stable feature is the ruthlessness of their punishments: in other words, the reign of terror.

FANATICISM VERSUS IDEALISM

The masses are fanatical rather than ideological (adhering to a firm set of political or economic principles) or idealist (aspiring, utopically, to moral or political perfection). Far more extreme than a mob, upon which fanaticism has a short-lived hold, the masses can fall under the spell of a charismatic evil leader even when it's no longer in their self-interest. How is this self-defeating attitude possible? Arendt explains: "identification with the movement and total conformism seem to have destroyed the very capacity for experience, even if it be as extreme as torture or fear of death" (*The Origins of Totalitarianism*, 308).

THE PHILISTINE VERSUS THE BOURGEOIS

Totalitarian movements transform ordinary human beings into philistines. Arendt describes "the philistine" as a bourgeois individual who is isolated from his class. The philistine focuses so much on his own narrow needs that he views victims as "Others" rather than as fellow human beings. "Nothing proved easier to destroy than the privacy and the private morality or people who thought of nothing but safeguarding their private lives," Arendt elaborates. "After a few years of power and systematic co-ordination, the Nazis could rightly announce: 'The only person who is still a private individual in Germany is somebody who is asleep'" (*The Origins of Totalitarianism*, 338–9). Decades after its publication, *The Origins of Totalitarianism* remains the most rigorous and systematic explanation of how such mass horrors could have occurred during the twentieth century. Arendt's book also serves as a necessary reminder that they can happen again for as long as humanity can be enchained by totalitarian regimes.

Chapter Fifteen

Beyond the Jewish Genocide

Inferno by Max Hastings

The Holocaust refers to the genocide of nearly six million Jews by the Nazis and their collaborators. There is no doubt that the Jews were singled out for systematic extermination. However, it is important to keep in mind that the Nazis murdered and sent to slave labor camps millions of non-Jews as well. Over three million Russians died as prisoners of war in the concentration and labor camps established by the Nazis.

Historian Max Hastings documents that by February 1942, "almost 60 percent of the 3.35 million Soviet prisoners in German hands had perished; by 1945, 3.3 million were dead out of 5.7 million taken captive" (*Inferno*, 488). A large percentage of Russian civilians sent to Nazi forced labor camps—170,000 out of 2.77 million workers—died there, along with large numbers of Polish and Italian prisoners of war (*Inferno*, 489).

The Nazi policy of deliberately starving the inhabitants of conquered territories (in Holland, Poland and parts of the Soviet Union) in order to channel food and supplies to their own soldiers and civilian population led to the slow and painful death of millions of innocent people. Auschwitz statistics tell a grim story about the Nazi regime's victims. According to Hastings, out of the over one million Jews who arrived at the camp only 100,000 survived, against all odds. Only half of the non-Jewish Polish prisoners survived in the camp. By the end of August 1944, when the Gypsy camp was liquidated, 2000 out of the 23,000 Gypsies incarcerated at Auschwitz made it out alive (*Inferno*, 486).

Ruth Maier, a young Jewish Austrian woman, considered this inclusive perspective of the Holocaust shortly before she herself was sent to a concentration camp:

> If you shut yourself away and look at this persecution and torture of Jews only from the viewpoint of a Jew, then you'll develop some sort of complex which is bound to lead to a slow but certain psychological collapse. The only solution is to see the Jewish question from a broader perspective.... We'll only be rich when we understand that it's not just we who are a race of martyrs. That beside us there are countless others suffering, who will suffer like us until the end of time ... if we don't ... fight for a better. (Cited in *The Diary of Ruth Maier*, translated by Jamie Bulloch, Vintage Books 2010)

Ruth never got the chance to finish her sentence. She perished at Auschwitz on December 1, 1942. Decades later, in 2010, her diary appeared in an English translation by Jamie Bulloch under the title of *Ruth Maier's Diary: A Jewish Girl's Life in Nazi Europe*. Some have compared her writing to that of Hannah Arendt and Susan Sontag. Others have likened it to the journal of Anne Frank. Ruth's diary offers an eloquent personal testimony about the Holocaust as well as an important universal message: The Holocaust targeted Jews first and foremost, but the Nazi ethnic cleansing claimed millions of lives and would have annihilated entire peoples and nations had Hitler's aims come to full fruition. Ethnic hatred poisons the lives of countless individuals, often reaching far beyond its initial group of victims.

Chapter Sixteen

Hitler's Ban on Modern Art

The "Degenerate Art" Exhibit

Artistic and political freedom usually go together. "Where books are burned, people are burned," declared the poet Heinrich Heine. Indeed, governments that ban art tend to also heavily restrict the freedom of speech and of the press. This holds as true for today's tyrannies as it did for the totalitarian regimes of the twentieth century. Not surprisingly, ISIL—the terrorist organization known as the Islamic State of Iraq and the Levant, which is responsible for publicized beheadings of innocent civilians, burning or stoning people to death, kidnapping and rapes—has implemented a *sharia* school in Mosul, a city it controls in Northern Iraq, where it has banned the teaching of art, music, history and literature.

During the Stalinist and post-Stalinist regimes in Eastern Europe, Communist states instituted the reign of Socialist Realism in the realm of culture. All artistic fields—the visual and plastic arts, music, theater, film, dance, and literature—became subordinated to the goal of glorifying Communist ideology and the "workers' revolution." In reality, of course, this meant reducing culture to a personality cult of the tyrant in power, thereby stifling creativity and the freedom of expression.

The Nazis followed a similar process. To spread Fascist ideology throughout German society, Hitler essentially banned most modern art, which his regime called "degenerate art" ("Entartete Kunst"), viewing it as a product of Jewish or Communist cultural corruption. Ironically, the term "Entartung" (or "degeneracy") was coined in 1892 by the Jewish author Max Nordau. It referred to the supposedly atavistic traits of "born criminals." When the Nazis rose to power, they used the concept of "degeneracy" to describe all aspects of culture they considered to be contaminated by "the perverse Jewish spirit."

By 1937, the works of Europe's most famous modern artists—the Dadaists, the Post-Impressionists (including Henri Matisse and Vincent Van Gogh), the Expressionists (Wassily Kandinsky, Paul Klee, Marc Chagall), the Abstract Expressionists (Pablo Picasso)—as well as some of the world's leading modernist writers (such as Ernest Hemingway and Thomas Mann) were purged from museums, libraries, and private collections. Over 5,000 works of modern art were confiscated.

In 1937, the Nazis, under the cultural leadership of Adolf Ziegler, head of the Reich Chamber of Visual Art, and of Joseph Goebbels, Reich Minister of Propaganda, created a travelling exhibit devoted to mocking so-called "degenerate art." It was first held in Munich on July 19, 1937, and later moved around to cities throughout Germany and Austria. A large and imposing portrait of Jesus greeted the crowds. To signal disrespect, modernist paintings were strewn about haphazardly and often left unframed, sometimes hanging only by a cord. The signs posted next to them expressed slogans that were intended to undermine their value. These epithets included "Revelation of the Jewish Racial Soul," "An Insult to German Womanhood," "The Ideal—cretin and whore," and "Nature as seen by sick minds." As Carole Strickland explains, "The object was to discredit any work that betrayed Hitler's master race ideology; in short, anything that smacked of dangerous free-thinking. Nazi leaders considered Modernist art so threatening they prohibited children from the show and hired actors to roam the halls loudly criticizing modern art as the work of lunatics. . . . Price tags displayed how much public museums had paid for the works with signs 'Taxpayer, you should know how your money was spent'" (*The Annotated Mona Lisa*, Andrew McMeel Publishing, Kansas City, 1992).

The plans to undermine modern art at the 1937 Munich "Degenerate Art" show backfired. Despite the Nazi attack, the exhibit of modernist works was extremely popular, attracting three million visitors. Unfortunately, in 1942 the Nazis burned, in the gardens of the Galerie Nationale du Jeu de Paume in Paris, countless modernist works by notable artists such as Picasso, Klee, Leger, and Miro. Their contempt for modern art didn't prevent them, however, from exploiting it for financial gain. The Nazis looted museums and private collections throughout occupied Europe as a means of enriching Germany at the expense of other European countries.

Chapter Seventeen

Saving European Art from the Nazis

The Monuments Men

One of the main cultural battles against Hitler and the Nazi regime during WWII was over art. Since Hitler's men pillaged museums and private collections and hid stolen works of art throughout Europe, the Allies were obliged to try to retrieve them. Franklin D. Roosevelt spearheaded this effort.

FDR had long supported the arts as an important part of the New Deal. The Federal Art Project (FAP) became the visual art component of the New Deal Works Progress (active between August 29, 1935, and June 30, 1943). Its goal was to revive the U.S. economy and overcome the effects of the Great Depression. The FAP encouraged public art of all kinds, including paintings, murals, and sculptures. It sought to bring art, once again, to the foreground in the country. Unlike Hitler, who repudiated modernism, Roosevelt maintained a pluralist stance, encouraging both representational and abstract art. FAP displayed, for instance, the works of Jackson Pollock long before abstraction became a mainstream art movement during the 1950s.

Hitler had his own art program and ambitions. A frustrated artist who was denied admission to the Vienna Academy of Fine Arts, he nonetheless pursued artistic goals once he attained power. Hitler wanted to create the world's greatest art museum, dedicated to himself, called the Führermuseum. During WWII, he pillaged many of Europe's best museums in the countries he conquered, as well as private collections owned by Jews and other people he sent to concentration camps. The art he stole and the art he destroyed reflected his particular taste as well as his intolerance for the tastes of others. He ordered that many of the masterpieces of Cubism, Futurism, and Dadaism be systematically destroyed. Launching a propaganda campaign against modern art, Joseph Goebbels called such art "garbage." On March 20, 1939,

Hitler ordered the Berlin Fire Department to burn over a thousand paintings and sculptures and over three thousand watercolors, drawings, and prints of modern art.

While repudiating modernist contemporary art, the Nazis coveted the masterpieces of the past. Pillaging conquered and occupied countries, they looted their museums and private collections. They surreptitiously shipped and hid the artworks in caves and private houses throughout Europe. Hitler's plan was to eventually display most of these stolen works in the Führermuseum. This massive museum was to be built in Linz, Austria, where Hitler spent most of his youth. After he rose to power, the city became a leading cultural center of the Third Reich.

In 1940, Hermann Göring, who was notorious for his greed and ostentatious wealth, ordered the Nazis to seize Jewish art collections (including those owned by very wealthy, prominent families such as Rothschilds, the Rosenbergs, and the Goudstikkers) and store them at the Musée Jeu de Paume in Paris before sending them to Germany. This operation was organized by the Einsatzstab Reichsleiter Rosenberg (or ERR, the Reischsleiter Rosenberg Institute for Occupied Territories, directed by Alfred Rosenberg), which dealt with the patrimony of countries under German control. Göring placed Bruno Lohse in charge of the Musée Jeu de Paume, its curators and staff. He supervised the shipping of artifacts to secret places in Belgium and Germany. Between 1940 and 1942, Göring traveled to Paris numerous times to oversee the shipment of art and artifacts. These looting operations, which included hundreds of thousands of works of art, spread to other conquered countries and regions around the world, including the Netherlands, Belgium, Russia, and North Africa.

The Allies took note of the plunder of European art by Nazi Germany and established their own agency, called the Monuments, Fine Arts and Archives (MFAA) organization, to protect the artwork from destruction by bombing and retrieve the stolen art objects. *The Monuments Men* (February, 2014), directed by George Clooney, with an all-star cast that includes Clooney himself, Matt Damon, Bill Murray, John Goodman, and Cate Blanchett, follows the efforts of several art connoisseurs—museum directors, curators, art historians, and architects—to enter the European combat zones during WWII and reclaim the artworks and private collections stolen by the Nazis. This entertaining and informative film is, in turn, based on Robert M. Edsel's best-seller *The Monuments Men: Allied Heroes, Nazi Thieves and the Greatest Treasure Hunt in History* (Center Street, New York, 2010).

Although *The Monuments Men* received mixed critical reviews, the movie deserves credit for reminding us of the value—and vulnerability—of art. Today the art world is threatened not only by war (as are the artifacts of Iraq for instance) but also by a growing public indifference to it. It seems that art and literature risk being replaced with entertainment. Artists, critics, movie producers, and actors thus face another challenge: making art and culture visible and relevant again to the general public.

Chapter Eighteen

The Holocaust in Austria and Woman in Gold

Until the 1930s, and particularly before the *Anschluss*, or Hitler's annexation in March 1938, the Jewish people thrived in Austria. However, like many other European countries, Austria experienced a rise in anti-Semitism during the 1930s. The country was home to approximately 200,000 Jews, most of whom lived in Vienna. They comprised about 9 percent of the capital's population. When the Nazis marched into the city, numerous Austrians greeted them with enthusiasm. Once Austria became part of the Third Reich, following a rigged plebiscite that indicated 99 percent of the country was in support of this union, the Nazis hastened to implement anti-Semitic legislation based on the Nuremberg Laws already in effect in Germany.

The anti-Jewish rallies, pogroms and laws that took years to consolidate in Germany swept over Austria in a matter of months. Jews were arrested on various pretexts. Their property and stores were looted; their synagogues were burned. Hundreds of them were sent to Dachau, a concentration camp in Germany and to Mauthausen, the newly established concentration camp in Austria. Many Jews tried to flee the country. Those who chose to stay or couldn't escape in time were eventually deported to various Jewish ghettos throughout Eastern Europe: particularly Minsk, Riga and Lodz. As the Ghettos were eventually liquidated, their inhabitants were sent to die in concentration camps. Thousands of Viennese Jews were sent to the Theresienstadt concentration camp in Czechoslovakia and later deported to Auschwitz. By 1942, fewer than 10,000 Jews remained in Austria. Most of them were saved by the fact that they were married to non-Jewish Austrians.

Right after the *Anschluss*, both Eichmann and Göring came to Vienna to speed up the implementation of anti-Semitic legislation. In a speech delivered on March 26, 1938, Göring stated that the Aryanization of Austria—

which entailed, among other things, the confiscation and redistribution of Jewish property to "Aryans"—must occur immediately and be carried out in an "absolutely systematic manner" (*The Holocaust*, 105). As Leni Yahil explains, the term "property" included "assets of all kinds: works of art, jewelry, even all types of commercial and social benefits" (*The Holocaust: The Fate of European Jewry, 1932–1945*, translated from Hebrew by Ina Friedman and Haya Galai, Oxford: Oxford University Press, 1990, 105).

This is the historical era that the film *Woman in Gold* (2015) captures. The movie, which is based on a true story, follows the legal and emotional struggles of an elderly Jewish Austrian woman living in the U.S., Maria Altmann (played by Helen Mirren), to reclaim a painting of her aunt Adele. This exquisite portrait is executed by the famous Art Nouveau painter Gustav Klimt. In 1907, the artist was commissioned by Adele's husband, Ferdinand Bloch-Bauer, a wealthy entrepreneur who made his fortune in the sugar industry, to paint several portraits of his beautiful wife.

After Adele died from meningitis in 1925, her husband discovered in her will that she wished to donate the Klimt painting to the Austrian State Gallery. Years later, to escape the Nazis, Ferdinand fled to Zurich. After the Anschluss, the Nazis seized his property, including the Klimt portrait of his wife. In 1941, the portrait of Adele was transferred to the Belvedere Palace in Vienna, owned by the Austrian State Gallery. Over the years, Klimt's gilded and elegant portrait of Adele Bloch-Bauer became one of Austria's most prized artistic possessions, with an estimated value of well over 100 million dollars.

When Maria tries to reclaim the painting, she finds that the Austrian government is not willing to part with it. Despite her reluctance to revisit the past and open old wounds, Maria is obliged to do just that. She hires a young lawyer, E. Randol Schoenberg (played by Ryan Reynolds), to help her take back her family's treasure. For her, this battle represents far more than a sentimental attachment to her aunt's portrait. It also symbolizes a belated form of justice for the countless Jewish people robbed by the Nazi regimes. After several court battles in the United States that take the case of the stolen artwork all the way to the Supreme Court, in 2006, Maria is able to win a binding arbitration decision in Austria.

Ronald S. Lauder, the President and co-founder of Neue Gallery in New York City, announced that he acquired the Adele Bloch-Bauer portrait for 135 million dollars. Lauder stated, "With this dazzling painting, Klimt created one of his greatest works of art. We are overjoyed to be able to give Adele Bloch-Bauer a permanent home at the Neue Galerie. Her presence will enrich the museum immeasurably" (Ronald S. Lauder, June 19, 2006). While some critics interpret the legal dispute for Klimt's famous portrait as an exercise in greed, I think that the movie rightly emphasizes the historical significance of reclaiming this magnificent work of art.

Chapter Nineteen

On the Anschluss

Becoming Alice

Hitler had strong ties to Austria. Born on April 20, 1889, in Braunau am Inn, Austria-Hungary (a little town close to Bavaria, Germany), Hitler returned in 1905 to his native country to study art in Vienna. His failure as an art student may have marked him for life. He was rejected from the Academy of Fine Arts twice, in 1907 and 1908, and even lived in a homeless shelter for a few months in 1909. Years later, after acquiring power in Germany, Hitler was determined to return to Austria as a triumphant leader. He fulfilled this dream when he marched into Austria on March 12, 1938, during the Anschluss. "Anschluss" literally means a "connection" or "union." This choice of wording was part of the Nazi propaganda campaign, to describe the annexation of Austria as a mutually beneficial arrangement rather than what it actually was: a German invasion and occupation of a sovereign country. The coup d'état enacted by the Austrian Nazi Party with German backing facilitated this "union."

The annexation of Austria, however, was by no means welcomed by all Austrians. The Nazis claimed that they received 99 percent of votes in support of the union in a plebiscite they held in the country following the invasion. In fact, the Austrian government had initially distanced itself from the Nazis, cutting economic ties with Germany once Adolf Hitler rose to power. Hitler, however, launched a powerful propaganda campaign to create the illusion of nearly unanimous Austrian support. On March 12, the German Wehrmacht crossed into Austria, greeted by large crowds of cheering citizens of German descent, who were holding flowers and waving Nazi flags.

Once in control of the country, the German Nazis suppressed all opposition. They arrested 70,000 people whom they perceived to be enemies of the

Nazi regime, targeting Jewish Austrians and Communists in particular for discrimination and abuse. The Anschluss was Hitler's first major show of force against an autonomous nation. The annexation of Austria would become a precedent for future German conquests, either "by flowers," as the Anschluss was called because it occurred without a fight, or through a declaration of war and forced occupation.

Alice Rene's *Becoming Alice: A Memoir* describes this important moment in twentieth-century history. Hailed as "a deftly written memoir that will hold the reader's attention from beginning to end" by the *Midwest Book Review* and as "a magnificent memoir and an impressive, courageous piece of work" by *Writers Digest Magazine*, Rene's memoir deserves its praise. The book begins with a detailed and personalized account of the Anschluss. *Becoming Alice* depicts the impact of these tragic historical events upon Austria's Jewish population from the perspective of a six-year-old girl named Isle.

Isle and her family watch helplessly as Nazi soldiers march down their street in Vienna. Faced with discrimination and the threat of deportation, they decide to flee Austria for fear of worse mistreatment. Taking only their most basic belongings, Isle and her father, mother, and older brother (Fredi) risk a difficult journey through Stalinist Russia. In an adventurous voyage, they eventually make their way to Portland, Oregon.

Alice Rene's autobiographical narrative skillfully captures the girl's perspective as she lives through one of the most inhumane and incomprehensible moments in history. While Isle and her family are extremely fortunate to have escaped the Holocaust, finding themselves as new immigrants in the United States is no easy matter. As Isle adapts to the new culture and craves acceptance and assimilation, she becomes increasingly critical of her family's dynamics—particularly of the interaction between her overbearing father and submissive yet, in some respects, also strong and resilient mother. By the end of the narrative, when she's already in her teens, Isle succeeds in Americanizing not only her name, which she changes to Alice, but also her identity. She never forgets, however, her family's original culture, nor the historical calamity that brought them to the United States.

Chapter Twenty

The Gypsy Holocaust

The Nazi Persecution of the Gypsies

The Gypsies also experienced a Holocaust at the hands of the Nazis. Initially, Nazi racial ideology expressed some ambivalence towards the Gypsies, by way of contrast to the Jews, whom they unequivocally perceived as "vermin." On the one hand, the Nazis regarded the Gypsies as "work-shy," nomadic beggars and thieves, racially inferior to the Aryan race. On the other hand, some Nazi racial theories traced the "racially pure" Gypsies to "Aryan" Indian tribes. In the end, this dual perspective didn't alter their mistreatment of the Gypsies. Although the Nazis didn't have a comparable "Final Solution," or systematic plan to exterminate them as a race, the Gypsies suffered a similar fate to the Jews. They were rounded up for slave labor, isolated in ghettos (or Gypsy Camps) and subsequently sent to killing centers. Guenter Lewy's book *The Nazi Persecution of the Gypsies* (Oxford: Oxford University Press, 2001) traces the oppression of the Gypsies in Germany and Nazi controlled territories, starting with the imposition of racial laws during the early 1930s, to their deportation to concentration camps beginning in 1940, to their eventual extermination at Auschwitz in May 1944.

When the Nazis consolidated power in 1936, Heinrich Himmler, who became the SS Chief and the Chief of German Police, instituted the *Reich Central Office for the Suppression of the Gypsies Nuisance*. This organization took progressive steps to contain and persecute the Gypsies. As early as 1938, Lewy recounts, the Gypsies were rounded up and confined to Gypsy camps (Zigeunerlager). Many men were also forced into slave labor, under the program "Operation Work-Shy." Himmler took charge of this step-by-step process. In a decree entitled "Combatting the Gypsy Plague," he set out to determine the "inner characteristics of that race" (36). Dr. Robert Ritter, a

Nazi child psychologist, became the head of *The Research Institute for Racial Hygiene and Population Biology*. He classified the Gypsies according to their racial profile, as purebred or mixed (43). Gypsies of "pure blood" received some special consideration and were deemed to be more integrated into German society. By way of contrast, "mixed blood" Gypsies were declared "racially inferior" and subjected to worse treatment, in an inversion of the Nazi racial laws applied to the Jews.

Only a small number of Gypsies, between 5,000 and 15,000 individuals, benefitted from the racial exemptions applicable to "pure Gypsies." The rest, about 90 percent of the Gypsy population, was considered by Ritter's pseudoscientific classification to be of "mixed" or "degenerate" blood. The vast majority of Gypsies were rounded up and deported from the Reich and from the Nazi-occupied territories. In 1938, Gypsy men from Marzahn were sent to Sachsanhausen. However, the large-scale mass deportations of the Gypsies to the East began later, in 1940. By 1942, Himmler issued an order that all the Gypsies (Roma people) in the Reich should be deported to concentration and extermination camps (75).

At Auschwitz, Gypsies were some of the few inmates, along with a group of Czech prisoners from the Theresienstadt concentration camp (known as "the Family Camp"), who were allowed to keep their civilian clothes, not shave their hair off, and stay together in clans and families that comprised men, women, and children. Despite the better treatment of Gypsies in some respects, their overall conditions were miserable. They lacked sufficient food, lived in squalor and were plagued by lice and disease. Gypsy children often suffered from noma, an illness stemming from malnutrition that caused gangrenes on their faces, which often took the form of holes in their cheeks. The notorious Josef Mengele preferred experimenting on Gypsy children, particularly on twins, his specialty.

Lewy doesn't call the Nazi persecution of the Gypsies a "Holocaust" because it was, in some respects, less systematic than the Jewish genocide. Gypsies were not explicitly selected for total extermination as were the Jewish people. In the end, however, the result was the same, since the vast majority of Gypsies—approximately 250,000 men, women, and children—were killed by the Nazi regime.

Chapter Twenty-One

Eichmann in Jerusalem

What is the Banality of Evil?

The biographical movie *Hannah Arendt* (2012), directed by Margarethe von Trotta and starring Barbara Sukowa, reveals that Arendt's series of articles about the trial of Adolf Eichmann, covered by *The New Yorker* in 1961 and subsequently published under the title *Eichmann in Jerusalem: A Report on the Banality of Evil* (Penguin Books, New York, 1963), was a double-edged sword for the author's career. On the one hand, the book increased Arendt's mainstream visibility, partly because of the international controversy it generated. On the other hand, this very controversy cost her several friendships and jeopardized her scholarly reputation for a while. The controversy centers upon the manner in which the author describes the nature of evil that characterizes the Holocaust.

Arendt's explanation, captured by the phrase "the banality of evil," posits that evil deeds are, for the most part, not perpetrated by monsters or sadists. Most often, they are perpetrated by seemingly "ordinary" people like Adolf Eichmann, who value conformity and self-interest over the welfare of others. The concept of the banality of evil seems intuitive enough. Nonetheless, it created an uproar in intellectual circles. Many critics interpreted Arendt's use of it as exonerating Adolf Eichmann and indicting the victims of the Holocaust: particularly the Jewish leaders who were compelled by the Nazis to organize their people for mass deportations and eventual extermination.

Was Arendt putting criminals and victims in the same boat? Or, worse yet, does her notion of the banality of evil end up blaming the victims? That depends upon how we interpret her argument. In what follows, I'd like to explore these questions by outlining Arendt's two main explanations of the banality of evil: the first one being people who lack empathy and conscience under any circumstances (like Eichmann) and the second understood as evil actions (or callous indifference) that even people who do have a conscience are capable of under extreme circumstances.

ADOLF EICHMANN AND THE BANALITY OF PSYCHOPATHY

Adolf Eichmann (1906–1962) was a Lieutenant Colonel in the Nazi regime and one of the key perpetrators of the Holocaust. With initiative and enthusiasm, he organized the mass deportations of Jews first to ghettos and then to extermination camps throughout Nazi-occupied Europe. Once Germany lost the war, Eichmann fled to Argentina. In 1960, he was captured by the Mossad (the Israeli National Intelligence Agency) and extradited to Israel. A year later, in a public trial, he was charged with crimes against humanity and war crimes. He was found guilty and executed by hanging.

In her account of Eichmann's trial, Arendt is struck by the contrast between this man's monstrous deeds and his average appearance and banal, technocratic language. Unlike other Nazi leaders notorious for their crimes against humanity, such as Amon Goeth or Josef Mengele, Eichmann didn't appear to be a sadist. More remarkably, given his atrocious actions against the Jewish people, unlike Hitler, Eichmann wasn't even particularly anti-Semitic.

Although six psychiatrists testified during the trial about Eichmann's apparent "normality," in her articles Arendt emphasizes that his apparent normalcy is only a mask. She highlights the aspects of Eichmann's behavior under questioning that are anything but normal: his self-contradictions, lies, evasiveness, denial of blame about the crimes he did commit and inappropriate boasting about his power and role in the Holocaust for crimes there's no evidence he committed. Arendt is particularly struck by this man's absolute lack of empathy and remorse for having sent hundreds of thousands of people to their deaths. To each count he was charged with, Eichmann pleaded "Not guilty in the sense of the indictment" (21). This leads Arendt to ask: "In what sense then did he think he was guilty" (21)? According to his defense attorney, "Eichmann feels guilty before God, not before the law" (21). In other words, this mass murderer never acknowledged any human wrongdoing.

If Eichmann denies culpability it's because, as Arendt is astonished to observe, he doesn't feel any moral responsibility for his crimes. Although, surprisingly, none of the forensic psychologists see him as a psychopath, Arendt describes Eichmann in similar terms that Hervey Cleckley uses to describe psychopathic behavior in his 1941 groundbreaking book *The Mask of Sanity*. First and foremost, he is a man with abnormally shallow emotions. Because of this, he also has no empathy and scruples. Even though he understands the concept of law, Eichmann has no visceral sense of right and wrong and doesn't care about the pain he inflicts upon others. His extraordinary emotional shallowness impoverishes not only his sense of ethics, but also his vocabulary. Arendt gives as one of many examples Eichmann's desire to "find peace with his former enemies" (53). She observes, "Eichmann's mind was filled to the brim with such sentences" (53). These stock phrases are a manifestation of Eichmann's empty emotional landscape, as his behavior towards the Jews amply confirms.

In a review of *Hannah Arendt* (the movie) that also focuses on *Eichmann in Jerusalem*, Mark Lilla argues that Hannah Arendt was duped by Eichmann's mask of sanity. He maintains that Arendt's search for a more general explanation of evil blinded her to Eichmann's personality disorder: "But the other impulse, to find a schema that would render the horror comprehensible and make judgment possible, in the end led her astray. Arendt was not alone in being taken in by Eichmann and his many masks, but she was taken in" (Mark Lilla, "Arendt and Eichmann: The New Truth," *The New York Review of Books*, November 21, 2013). In her description of Eichmann as a man without conscience and empathy, I see Arendt as regarding him as a psychopath, even though she never uses this clinical term. If evil is banal it's only because psychopathy itself is prevalent enough to make a big historical impact upon ordinary people's lives. At any rate, I would agree with Mark Lilla's observation that Eichmann himself was far from ordinary. His lack of empathy was exceptional, while his pathological callousness was only thinly disguised by a mask of sanity.

Yet, Arendt emphasizes, even ordinary people capable of empathy and remorse can cause great harm in extraordinary circumstances. This constitutes the second understanding of the banality of evil she develops—namely, the banality of conformity.

HANNAH ARENDT ON THE DANGERS OF CONFORMITY

The controversy surrounding Hannah Arendt's *Eichmann in Jerusalem: A Report on the banality of evil* also centers upon the perception that the author blamed the Jewish leaders for being coerced to play an active role in the Holocaust. Arendt states, "To a Jew this role of the Jewish leaders in the destruction of their own people is undoubtedly the darkest chapter in the whole dark story" (117). She goes on to argue, "The whole truth was that if the Jewish people had really been unorganized and fearless, there would have been chaos and plenty of misery but the total number of victims would hardly have been between four and a half and six million people" (125). In my opinion, this statement constitutes a factual observation rather than a moral indictment. It was common knowledge, long before Arendt pointed it out, that the Nazis used local Jewish leaders to create Jewish Councils in countries under Nazi control. It was equally well known that the role of the Jewish Councils was to round up the Jews in ghettos, govern them temporarily and write up the lists of the selected groups of victims who were to be deported to labor or concentration camps.

Yet Arendt doesn't cast moral blame upon these misfortunate Jewish leaders. She acknowledges that they were largely motivated by a mixture of fear, incomplete knowledge (of Hitler's ultimate plans) and wishful thinking. They hoped that by cooperating with the Nazis they could appease the enemy and save at least part of the local Jewish population from harm. For the most part, those proved to be false hopes. However, it's worth noting that in some rare cases, the appeasement policies of the Jewish leaders did pay off. To offer one noteworthy example, Benjamin Murmelstein, the elder of the Judenrat in the Theresienstadt concentration camp (after 1943), was able to protect thousands of Jews by facilitating their emigration.

Arendt also states that those who have never been placed in such an impossible situation shouldn't throw stones at those who were. Some asked the victims, "Why did you not protest?" (11) She points out the insensitivity of this question, which rests upon the implicit value judgment that the victims could and should have protested. In that oppressive context, almost nobody did. "But the sad truth of the matter," Arendt observes, "is that the point was ill taken, for no non-Jewish group or people had behaved differently" (11). This is an important point, since non-Jews not only greatly outnumbered Jews—which means their protests would have carried more force—but also they were not as oppressed, so they would have had more opportunities to object and resist.

I believe that Arendt doesn't indict the Jewish leaders for their (coerced) complicity in the Holocaust, as some claim, but rather offers a general warning about the dangers of gradual acquiescence to nefarious policies. One of the most striking examples she offers of the evil of conformity is the Nazi conference focused on the implementation of the Final Solution. On January 20, 1942, the Nazi leaders, under the direction of Reinhard Heydrich (the head of the RSHA, Reich Main Security Office), attended a conference in a villa in Wannsee, a Berlin suburb, to discuss plans for the Final Solution. They weren't debating whether or not to exterminate the Jewish people. Hitler had already decided this matter. The main question they addressed was how to kill so many people, where to do it and how to transport the victims most efficiently to death camps. The Nazi leaders calmly discussed the logistics of killing millions of individuals, as if planning genocide were just another day at the office. None of them voiced any moral objections or even mentioned humanitarian considerations. This meeting sealed the fate of the Jews. Yet the Nazi leaders treated it as a routine administrative matter and networking opportunity—in Arendt's words, as "a cozy little social gathering" (113).

Arendt also offers the Danish people as an important counterexample. They refused on principle to adopt immoral measures against the Jews. "What happened then," she observes, "was truly amazing; compared with what took place in other European countries, everything went topsy-turvy" (172). The Danish military commanders rejected the Nazi discriminatory laws against the Jews on humanitarian grounds. Even Dr. Werner Best, the SS military commander sent over by Hitler to Denmark to oversee these anti-Semitic policies, refused to implement them.

Still discussing the principled position of the Danes, Arendt returns to the question of the role of the Jewish leaders. She shows that Jews who had the support of the local non-Jewish population—and thus some genuine hope of saving their people through resistance—did, indeed, behave courageously. The Dutch Jewish leaders refused to round up fellow Jews for deportation. They even forewarned people in synagogues about the precise times when the SS would go door to door to seize Jews and deport them. Faced with widespread opposition, even the local SS leaders lost their "toughness" on the Jewish question.

The exceptional case of Denmark in the history of the Holocaust shows, according to Arendt, "That the ideal of 'toughness,' except, perhaps, for a few half-demented brutes, was nothing but a myth of self-deception, concealing a ruthless desire for conformity at any price" (175). Evil actions often stem from the indifference or downright cooperation of a large number of ordinary individuals with inhumane orders designed by a few powerful evil leaders. Because it doesn't take much initiative to conform—sometimes the failure to protest proves enough—the "banality of evil" continues to pose a real danger for any country in any era. It takes pathological individuals like Hitler, Himmler, Stalin, or Eichmann to lead the masses to evil deeds. When the masses follow those leaders, ordinary conformity can cause extraordinary harm.

Chapter Twenty-Two

The Real Banality of Evil

Ordinary Men by Christopher R. Browning

As we've seen in the previous chapter, Hannah Arendt referred to Adolf Eichmann as the paradigm of the banality of evil—an ordinary man led by extraordinary circumstances to cause exceptional harm to others. However, given that Eichmann spearheaded some of the key initiatives of the murder of six million Jews during the Holocaust, I have argued that this malevolent man was quite extraordinary—essentially, a psychopath. The circumstances of Fascist Germany allowed Eichmann's personality disorder to be manifested through government-sanctioned murderous actions.

In *Ordinary Men: Reserve Police Battalion 101 and the Final Solution in Poland* (New York: Harper Perennial, 1993), historian Christopher R. Browning reveals the true nature of the banality of evil by recounting the transformation of members of the Order Police, the Police Battalion 101, from regular men to brutal mass murderers. Although initially the Order Police was composed of young men sympathetic to Nazi principles, by the late 1930s it included older men from all walks of life, including policemen, workers, and small businessmen. Browning notes that these Order Police units expanded during the war: "Twenty-one police battalions of approximately 500 men each were formed from the various police companies and training units in Germany, thirteen of them were attached to the armies invading Poland" (6).

While one can plausibly argue that the SS were chosen for their anti-Semitic ideology and brutality, that doesn't hold true in the case of Reserve Police Battalion 101. Yet this unit of five hundred "ordinary men" is responsible for the murder of 38,000 Jews and the deportation of an additional 45,200 in occupied Poland in 1942. Few of the perpetrators were tried for their crimes against humanity after the war. For those who did face a trial, their main defense was similar to Eichmann's: namely, that they were merely following the orders issued by their superiors. In their situation, unlike in Eichmann's (who occupied a Nazi leadership position), this defense seemed more or less plausible.

Few of these individuals were ardent Nazis. Even fewer had violent or sadistic tendencies. Most of them were middle-aged men no longer eligible for military duty. They were sent to Poland to participate in Operation Reinhard, to carry out the mass shootings of the Jewish populations of entire small towns, such as Jozefow and Lomazy. They did so voluntarily, although initially not eagerly. Most of these men hesitated to kill women and children in the beginning. Browning points out that, contrary to the later excuse they offered that they were merely following commands, these orders didn't entail any serious repercussions for those who refused to follow them. The commander of Unit 101 gave his soldiers the opportunity to opt out of conducting mass murders if they lacked the "fortitude" to kill women and children. All they faced, at worst, was peer pressure from some of their more ruthless colleagues. And yet, Browning notes, remarkably, only 12 out of the 500 men in Reserve Police Battalion 101 chose not to kill innocent people.

Seeing themselves as merely doing their duty, the Order Police rounded up and shot tens of thousands of helpless civilians. As they got used to their "job," they became more violent and sadistic. Some even smashed Jewish babies against the wall, or threw them up in the air and used them for target practice. Almost all of them became used to the mass murders, quickening the pace of slaughter and increasing their brutality as time went on. If any book can show that genocide can happen anywhere and be perpetrated by normal individuals placed in extraordinary circumstances, it is Browning's well-researched and persuasive historical account of the murderous actions of *Ordinary Men*.

Chapter Twenty-Three

Eichmann's Extraordinary Evil

Eichmann Before Jerusalem

In *Eichmann Before Jerusalem: The Unexamined Life of a Mass Murderer* (New York: Random House 2014), Bettina Stangneth challenges Hannah Arendt's hypothesis that Eichmann represents the banality of evil—namely, the assertion we examined earlier that Eichmann was an ordinary man turned mass murderer by extraordinary circumstances (WWII and the rise of Nazi totalitarianism). The image of Eichmann that emerges from Stangneth's book is one of a charming chameleon that deceives others about his intentions and credentials. Without knowing more than a few words of Yiddish and having virtually no knowledge of Hebrew, Eichmann relied upon the smattering of Jewish culture he got by spying on Jewish leaders to climb up the political ladder and obtain an official function as Head of Department of Jewish Affairs in the SD (the Security Service of the Nazi Party). Although most of the time he gave the impression of being calm and reserved, Eichmann would fly into a rage when his objectives were frustrated or when it served his purposes (such as to intimidate the Jewish leaders into complying with his orders). As if with the flip of a switch, however, he could instantly revert to being courteous, calm, and collected.

Eichmann's emotions, along with his attachments, were shallow. Although he remained, in some respects, "loyal" to his wife, Veronika Liebl, he cheated on and dominated her. At one point, he boasted that he tore up the Bible of his very religious wife, though eventually he "allowed her" to practice Christianity. Their bond remained strong in spite of her mistreatment. Vera waited patiently for years while Eichmann lived in hiding after the war. She eventually joined him in Argentina, where he managed to escape justice for eleven years.

The picture of Eichmann that emerges from Stangneth's book is, as I've suggested in my earlier discussion of Arendt's book, that of a psychopath—a highly narcissistic man without remorse, without conscience, and without the capacity to form deeper human attachments. Hungry for power, Eichmann adapted to the norms of the Nazi regime, even anticipating Hitler's wishes to implement a program of exterminating the Jews after the German invasion of Russia in 1941. War enabled the Nazis to perpetrate what couldn't be achieved during peacetime: a systematic genocide of unprecedented proportions carried out, at least in the Eastern campaign, openly and often with the cooperation of local populations.

Eichmann became partly responsible for the mass deportations of nearly six million Jews to concentration camps, where most of the victims were sent to the gas chambers. Far from merely following orders—as he later stated during his defense in the Jerusalem trial—Eichmann showed great enthusiasm and initiative for mass murder. In 1944, even Himmler had begun to reverse course and issued an order to stop the Jewish genocide in order to facilitate favorable peace negotiations for Germany with the Allies. Eichmann, however, went to Hungary to oversee the deportation and extermination of the Hungarian Jews. With astonishing efficiency, in a matter of months, he managed to send 437,000 Hungarian Jews to Auschwitz, where about 80 percent were killed on the spot and most of the rest died afterwards from hunger, abuse or disease.

As we've seen in previous chapters, the heroic actions of the Swedish diplomat Raoul Wallenberg prevented him from sending the Jews of Budapest to their deaths as well. Like many psychopaths, Eichmann was a bully with those in a position of weakness and weak with those in a position of strength. When Wallenberg confronted him face to face and stopped the deportation of hundreds of Jews, Eichmann didn't react. Only afterwards, behind his back, he railed against Wallenberg, calling him "a Jewish dog" and "an interventionist." Turning moral norms upside down, Eichmann felt that all those who expedited mass murder were courageous heroes while those who fought against it were cowards.

Eichmann remained, to the end, a man without conscience. After the war he even expressed great pride in his genocidal actions, claiming that he would "leap laughing into the grave because the feeling that he had five million people on his conscience would be for him a source of extraordinary satisfaction." Although he may have boasted about his murderous actions, Eichmann didn't want to suffer their consequences. After Germany's defeat in 1945, he fled to Austria and later, in 1950, to Argentina. There he joined a community of Nazi expatriates. Far from leading a quiet, anonymous life in hiding, this mass murderer longed for his former genocidal glory.

Emboldened by freedom, Eichmann even planned to write a book, based on a series of interviews with Willem Sassen, a Dutch collaborator and Nazi journalist also living in Argentina. This autobiography would not only leave his Nazi legacy for posterity but also, he hoped, instigate a second coming of the Third Reich during his lifetime. Eichmann's extraordinary hubris eventually destroyed him. The Mossad caught up with him in 1960 and brought him to Jerusalem to stand trial. He was charged with war crimes, crimes against humanity and crimes against the Jewish people. The jury found Eichmann guilty on all counts. He was executed by hanging on May 31, 1962.

Chapter Twenty-Four

The Concentration Camp Commandants

Soldiers of Evil

Thomas Segev's dissertation *Soldiers of Evil* (Jerusalem: Domino Press, 1987) goes a long way in explaining the psychology and social background of some of the Holocaust's most ruthless mass murderers, the concentration camp Commandants. The book relies upon eyewitness accounts, victim testimonials, court documents as well as interviews with some of the Commandants themselves, their acquaintances, colleagues, and family members who were willing to talk about the Nazi past. Segev notes that during Oswald Pohl's trial (he was the SS Commander in charge of administering the entire Nazi concentration camp system) it was estimated that the Nazis imprisoned about ten million people (*Soldiers of Evil*, 15). By the end of the war, in January 1945, only 700,000 were found alive by the Allies. Of those, tens of thousands died shortly after liberation. Close to one million non-Jewish prisoners and six million Jewish prisoners were killed in the Nazi extermination camps.

One might expect that those who directed the mass murder of millions of innocent people would be prone to sadism. Yet, in his study, Segev observes that this was true only in some exceptional cases. Certainly men like Amon Goeth, the Commandant of Plascow (vividly described by Thomas Keneally in *Schindler's List*), qualifies as sadistic. Goeth would notoriously go on random shooting sprees of defenseless inmates weakened by hard labor and hunger. Sometimes he would sic his dogs upon them to tear them apart limb from limb. Goeth enjoyed the process of selecting his victims and witnessing their torment. His widow, Ruth Kalder, a woman with sadistic tendencies herself, became enchanted with Goeth's cruelty. She claimed that it gave Goeth the aura of a God, as he wielded the power of life and death over Plascow's helpless inmates. After the war, she described her life with Goeth in the concentration camp in idyllic terms, comparing her husband and herself to the King and Queen of a fiefdom. Like Goeth, she showed no empathy for prisoners, particularly the Jews, whom she considered subhuman. In an interview she gave in 1975, Kalder stated, "They were not human like us.... They were so foul" (*Soldiers of Evil*, 201).

Likewise, Arthur Rodl, the Deputy Commandant to Karl Koch at Buchenwald concentration camp, enjoyed killing inmates with his bare hands. Segev recounts that on January 1, 1939, Rodl forced several thousand prisoners to line up. He then selected five among them, ordered them to strip and proceeded to whip them until morning to the sound of the camp orchestra (*Soldiers of Evil*, 133). The Commandant of Buchenwald, Karl Koch (known as "the monster of Buchenwald") and his wife, Isle, were also notorious for their cruelty to inmates. They lived at Buchenwald in a gorgeous mansion known as "Villa Koch," pampered like royalty in the midst of the squalor and misery of the concentration camp. The couple took great pleasure in abusing and killing prisoners. Segev recounts that Isle would dress up in a provocative manner and ride around the camp on horseback. If any of the inmates looked at her, she would sometimes beat them or, more commonly, ask her husband or the SS men to savagely attack them while she watched. Eventually the Nazi government tried Karl Koch not for his cruelty to prisoners (which was extreme even by Nazi standards) but for stealing goods—the money, jewelry, clothes, and extracted gold teeth—that the Nazi regime had confiscated from the Jews.

Despite such notorious examples of sadistic behavior, Segev's research indicates that the Commandants of the Nazi concentration camps had diverse social and psychological backgrounds. Most of them were not predisposed to sadism. However, they all underwent a powerful ideological conditioning. They also shared a propensity to dehumanize others and lacked empathy. As Segev observes, "There were among them men of different types: bureaucrats, opportunists, sadists, and criminals. The great majority of them were political soldiers" (*Soldiers of Evil*, 124). He further notes that most of them "saw themselves first and foremost as soldiers: two thirds of them had served in the army before joining the Nazi party and the SS. Most of them had volunteered for the army before, during, and after the First World War" (*Soldiers of Evil*, 60). For many, their experiences of the war served to desensitize them to human suffering and to habituate them to the act of killing. Some received special ideological training in Theodor Eicke's *Death's Head* squads. This was an elite formation in which Eicke, described by Segev as a "Nazi grand seigneur," recruited young men with Aryan features whom he indoctrinated with a toxic combination of Romantic nationalism, Nazi ideology and rabid anti-Semitism.

Perhaps the most revealing inside look into the concentration camp Commandants' mentality are the testimonies of Rudolf Hoss, the Commandant of Auschwitz, and of Franz Stangl, the Commandant of Treblinka. Neither of these men was particularly drawn to violence yet both of them killed hundreds of thousands of human beings. In his 1971 interview with the British writer and historian Gitta Sereny, Stangl is asked how he could have murdered so many people. He nonchalantly compares Jewish inmates to a herd of cattle trapped in their pins and headed for slaughter. Sereny asks him: "So you didn't feel they were human beings?" Stagl responds: "Cargo. They were cargo" (*Soldiers of Evil*, 201–2).

Rudolf Hoss, responsible for the deaths of nearly 2 million Jews at Auschwitz, dehumanized his victims in a similar fashion. In a conversation with his brother-in-law, Fritz Hensel, during the latter's four-week visit to Auschwitz, Hensel asks him how he could kill human beings. Hoss responds that the Jews were subhuman (Untermensch). Hensel asks for a clarification of the term "subhuman." According to his account, Hoss sighs and replies, "You always ask and ask. . . . Look, you can see for yourself. They are not like you and me. They are different. They look different. They do not behave like human beings. They have numbers on their arms. They are here in order to die" (*Soldiers of Evil*, 211). Using circular reasoning, the concentration camp Commandants dehumanized the Jews (as well as other groups of prisoners) through their deprivation and extremely cruel and inhumane treatment, then saw the results of their dehumanization as proof that their victims weren't fully human. Although most of them were not sadists, they could be exceptionally callous and cruel for ideological reasons and political gain.

Segev's research indicates that sadistic Commandants like Goeth and Koch did not meet the SS ideal. Their evil actions could not be controlled and channeled to serve the Nazi agenda. They killed for their own pleasure and stole for their own profit. The most successful concentration camp Commandants were those like Hoss and Stangl, "political soldiers" who killed millions of innocent human beings without conscience or remorse to fulfill the needs and ideals of the Nazi regime.

Chapter Twenty-Five

The Auschwitz Kommandant

Arthur Wilhelm Liebehenschel

Arthur Wilhelm Liebehenschel is often contrasted to Rudolf Höss to indicate that, relatively speaking, he was the "good" or "more humane" Commandant of Auschwitz. Liebehenschel ruled the notorious concentration camp from December 1943 to May 1944. His daughter from his first marriage, Barbara Cherish, does everything to exonerate his tarnished image and establish a rosier picture of his deeds in her memoir, *The Auschwitz Kommandant: A Daughter's Search for the Father She Never Knew* (United Kingdom: The History Press, 2009). There is no doubt that Liebehenschel was regarded as less brutal than Rudolf Höss. After taking over leadership of Auschwitz from Höss, he eliminated the notorious "standing cells," where prisoners were punished by being forced to stand for days, without food and water, in rooms smaller than a closet. He also put a stop to the selections of regular prisoners who were already in the concentration camp. While the sadistic punishment of inmates, particularly the Jews, was (at the very least) tolerated by Höss, Liebehenschel took steps to discourage the most severe punishments and forms of torture of camp inmates. According to Hermann Langbein, a prisoner in the Auschwitz infirmary, "in general one could establish that even those SS members who were very bloodthirsty before became a bit more reserved because they realized that their fanaticism would not necessarily be tolerated anymore."

Perhaps Liebehenschel's reputation for relative "leniency" played a role in his transfer from Auschwitz in the spring of 1944 and replacement with the previous Commandant, Rudolf Höss. Known for his callousness and efficiency, Höss was called back to Auschwitz to facilitate the extermination of over 400,000 Hungarian Jews deported to the concentration camp during the spring and summer of 1944. Liebehenschel was put in charge of the Majdanek extermination camp (outside Lublin) in May 1944. Although initially a labor camp rather than a death camp, Majdanek was transformed into an extermination camp of enormous proportions once Operation Reinhard (October 1941–November 1943), which stipulated the mass murder of all Jews in occupied Poland (General Government), was put into effect. At the end of WWII, Liebehenschel was arrested by the American Army and imprisoned for a short while in Dachau (under conditions that he himself described as humane). He was later extradited to Krakow to stand trial for crimes against humanity. Like Höss, he was found guilty and sentenced to death by hanging on January 28, 1948. Evidently, the law didn't distinguish between his crimes and those of Höss. Should we?

Reading the obviously biased memoirs of a daughter in search of her own identity by delving into her father's dark past raises the following question: Is there a real difference between men like Rudolf Höss and men like Arthur Liebehenschel, between "harsh" and "more humane" SS leaders? Although this memoir is meant to raise such a question in the reader's mind, in my opinion, the answers it provides aren't very satisfying. Cherish essentially exonerates her father. She apologies for his murderous deeds and, to some extent, even glosses over the outright lies he told the court in Krakow when he testified that he didn't know about the crematoria in either Auschwitz or Majdanek and wasn't in any way involved in the mass murders. Cherish's memoir therefore offers an extremely partial version of her father's life and reflects a deeply flawed moral perspective. There was no way one could be a so-called humane Auschwitz commander. This is a contradiction in terms. There was nothing humane about prisoners' lives in a lethal Nazi concentration camp.

However, just as there were differences in attitude and behavior among the SS officers at the camp—some of whom did their "job" with relish in punishing the prisoners, others who tried to avoid or minimize the punishments—the same can be said about the differences between Höss and Liebehenschel. This doesn't in any way excuse the mass murders committed by either of these men. If we draw a distinction between the two Auschwitz commandants, it's only to better grasp Hannah Arendt's notion of the "banality of evil." As previously noted, I believe that there was nothing commonplace or "banal" about the evil of men like Eichmann, whom she uses as her main example of this concept in *Eichmann in Jerusalem*, or of men like Höss. These two Nazi leaders exemplified *extraordinary evil*, going above and beyond the call of duty. Both individuals, in fact, played a significant role in masterminding the extermination of almost half a million of Hungarian Jews during a time when it was evident that Germany had already lost the war.

In my estimation, the concept of "the banality of evil" as elaborated by Arendt applies better to men such as Arthur Liebehenschel than to Adolf Eichmann. His daughter's claim that Liebehenschel didn't like to witness death and violence, learned mostly second-hand from her correspondence with Anneliesse (her father's second wife), is corroborated to some extent by Auschwitz survivors' testimonies. At the same time, the Auschwitz Kommandant oversaw the deaths of thousands of innocent human beings, who spent their last days in conditions that were, in themselves, sheer torture even if actual physical torture was discouraged.

Furthermore, according to Cherish's own account, Liebehenschel was a fervent Nazi; otherwise he could not have risen in the ranks of the SS. In different times, Arthur Liebehenschel might have played a role in better causes. In Nazi Germany, however, his ambition and misplaced loyalty to Hitler's regime led him to play a significant role in "the banality of evil"— namely, in committing gravely immoral acts against tens of thousands of innocent human beings, without any particular hatred for the victims or penchant for violence.

Chapter Twenty-Six

The Real Story of the Terezin Jewish Ghetto

I Am a Star

In some respects, Terezin (Theresienstadt), a concentration camp set up by the Nazis in November 1941 in Prague, was presented to the world as a "model community" of Jews. Hitler used Terezin in a Nazi propaganda campaign, to show the international community that the deported Jews were treated well, and sent to their own city, supposedly in order to protect them from external aggression and the dangers of war. The Terezin Jewish Ghetto was known as the "old people's" camp because many elderly Jews were sent there. It was also a place where the relatively privileged were interned: Jewish artists, writers and community leaders. Inge Auerbacher's Holocaust memoir, *I Am a Star: Child of the Holocaust* (New York: Puffin Books, 1986), reveals that this "model Jewish city," though perhaps not as lethal as the death camps, was a far cry from the idyllic Jewish community depicted by Nazi propaganda.

Nearly 150,000 men, women, and children were sent to this fortress town in Czechoslovakia. The Jewish Virtual Library documents that about a hundred thousand of them died there. Among them, 15,000 were children. Only about 240 children under the age of 15 survived. Inge Auerbacher was one of the fortunate few young adults who lived to reveal the truth about a walled-in prison where inmates suffered from hunger, disease, and the constant, rational, fear that they'd be sent to Auschwitz or Treblinka in the next wave of deportations.

Inge's memoir consists of a unique combination of her childhood memories of the camp, her poetry and her drawings of day-to-day life. The poetry is both evocative and informative. It describes life in this prison camp as well as her state of mind. Terezin was unique among the Jewish camps in keeping families together, at least for a period of time, and in not killing Jewish children right away. To offer just one example among many of the heart-wrenching poems in the book, "Deportation" describes her family's fear and sense of rootlessness once the deportations to Auschwitz began: "It was a morning like no other, The deadly letter was opened by Mother. She screamed out with a loud cry: 'It is true, we can no more deny, We are no longer citizens with a name, Now a transport number replaces the same'" (30).

Terezin was once a fortress built in 1780 by Joseph II to ward off invasions. The King named the city after his mother, Maria Teresa. Hitler subsequently transformed the old fortress into a prison for Jews, which he would use as a false cover for his murderous campaign against Europe's Jewish communities. The author describes the chasm between the Nazi propaganda campaign and reality. One of the drawings in the book features a group of gaunt, starving children sleeping head to toe, sometimes four to a narrow bed with soiled sheets. She recalls, "People died like flies in Terezin" from starvation, overwork and disease. "Papa became a scavenger, rummaging every day in the garbage dump in search of potato peelings and rotten turnips" (51). Overall, however, the living conditions in Terezin were not as severe as in the death camps. When the international Red Cross requested permission to visit a concentration camp following rumors of deportations of Jews to the East towards the end of 1943, the Nazis chose this fortress as their show camp. Inge recounts how part of the camp underwent a rapid makeover, in preparation for the Red Cross visit, which took place on June 23, 1944:

> Certain parts of the camp were cleaned up. Some people were given new clothing and good food to eat. A few children received chocolates and sardine sandwiches just as the commission walked past them. . . . The areas filled with the things that had been stolen from us were carefully locked up. Blind, crippled, and sick people were warned to stay out of sight. Even the most brutal SS officer, Rudolf Haindl, acted friendly on that day. (56–57)

The ruse worked. The Red Cross officials left believing Terezin was a model community for Jews. Eventually, however, all of its inmates were boarded up in cattle trains and sent to concentration and death camps. As Inge puts it, "Terezin was the antechamber to Auschwitz" (58). Adolf Eichmann took charge personally of planning these deportations. In Auschwitz, the inmates lived for a while in another so-called "model" camp, established on September 8, 1943, known as the "Family Camp."

Men and boys occupied even-numbered barracks; women and children odd-numbered ones. Unlike in most of Auschwitz (excluding the Gypsy Camp), the inmates could keep their regular clothes and didn't have their heads shaved. They could therefore preserve, to some extent, the semblance of normal life: "normal" only by comparison to the worse conditions that pervaded Auschwitz. But even they weren't safe from extermination.

Between July 10 and 12, 1944, 7,000 members of the Family Camp were savagely beaten by the SS and shoved into the gas chambers. Only a few protected Jews, primarily consisting of German WWI veterans and their families (which included Inge's family), were spared from this horrible fate. Ruth, the author's best friend, perished along with almost everyone else. Inge Auerbacher's memoir tells the real story of Terezin, the Jewish Ghetto created to serve Nazi propaganda. The book also pays a moving homage to Ruth and "so many other children as they marched with their mothers to the gas chambers in Auschwitz and the other extermination camps" (64).

Chapter Twenty-Seven

The Wannsee Conference

Planning the Final Solution

On January 20, 1942, fifteen high-ranking Nazi officials assembled at a villa located at 56-58 Am Grossen Wannsee near Berlin to plan the mass murder of the European Jews. Arriving in style in a Mercedes, Reinhard Heydrich, the Chief of the Reich Security Main Office (RHSA), indicated to the panelists that Hitler had personally entrusted him with implementing the "Final Solution" to Europe's "Jewish problem." The genocide was supposed to include not only the Jews living under Axis control or occupation, but also those living in Allied and neutral states, including citizens of the United Kingdom, Ireland, Sweden, Switzerland, Spain, and Portugal. According to the U.S. Holocaust Memorial Museum, the following Nazi officials representing the SS were present at this conference: Reinhard Heydrich, SS Lieutenant Colonel Adolf Eichmann, chief of the RSHA Department IV B4 (Jewish Affairs); SS Colonel Eberhard Schongarth, the commander of the RSHA field office in Krakow; SS Major Rudolf Lange, commander of Einsatzkommando 2 in Latvia; SS Major General Otto Hofmann, chief of SS Race and Settlement Office (see "Wannsee Conference and the 'Final Solution'").

These men were the leading architects of the world's biggest genocide. Remarkably, they treated the conference—and their decision—as an ordinary, productive and pleasant get-together. Nobody voiced any objections to killing millions of innocent men, women, and children. In fact, by the time the Wannsee conference took place, tens of thousands of Jews in the Nazi-occupied areas of the Soviet Union had already been rounded up and murdered, often with help from the local populations. The conference focused on how to expand this mass murder to the rest of Europe in the most effective fashion. If there was any debate among these men, it was regarding the logistics of transporting millions of people to their deaths. They also discussed what to do with German Jews in mixed marriages so that the general population wouldn't object to their mistreatment.

If you've read descriptions of criminals committing horrific murders and afterward going out to dinner with their families or playing with their children as if nothing unusual had taken place, then you'll be able to imagine these Nazi officials' cold and calculated mindset. Alex Kershaw paints a vivid picture of the Wannsee meeting in *The Envoy* (New York, Da Capo Press, 2010), a book that offers a historical account of Raoul Wallenberg's courageous actions to save the Jews of Budapest. After the Nazi leaders made the arrangements for mass murder, Kershaw narrates,

> Servants brought in refreshments. The attendees drank and ate and talked about finally ending the Jewish problem not just in Germany, but in all of Europe, including Britain and the Soviet Union. . . . The meeting formally ended after ninety minutes, with Heydrich and the Gestapo chief Heinrich Muller being the last to leave the large dining room. They asked the thorough Eichmann to share a drink with them. Soon the three men were beside a fire, warming themselves. Eichmann would never forget how honored he felt to be asked to join these two giants of the Third Reich for a celebratory tipple. . . . "After awhile," recorded Eichmann, "we got up on the chairs and drank a toast, then on the table and then round and round—on the chairs and on the table again. Heydrich taught it to us. It was an old north German custom. . . . We sat around peacefully after the Wannsee Conference, not just talking shop but giving ourselves a rest after so many taxing hours." (5–6)

Eichmann's casual account of the Wannsee conference and of the attitude of the men who participated in it speaks volumes about the Nazi regime and its power structure. The people who rose within its ranks were individuals without emotional depth, without empathy and without conscience. They did not care that millions of innocent people would die senselessly because of their decisions. In fact, they took great pride in the outcome of their meeting, indulging in pleasurable pastimes like smoking and drinking, to celebrate a "job" well done.

Chapter Twenty-Eight

America First

If any country could have saved a significant proportion of European Jews from the Holocaust it was the United States. Reliable news about concentration and death camps started trickling into the country in 1942 via the World Jewish Congress and the State Department. Moreover, the United States had a large number of Jews who, unlike the European and Soviet Jews, were free from the Nazi threat. American Jews did not face annihilation. As the United States did not have a significant Nazi movement, Jews in the United States, numbering approximately 4,800,000 million, could hope to influence public policy. Most American Jews supported President Roosevelt. Granted, few Jews in the United States were rich and powerful and only one—Henry Morgenthau, the U.S. Secretary of Treasury—was a prominent figure in the Roosevelt administration. Nevertheless, as Raul Hilberg documents in *Perpetrators, Victims, Bystanders* (HarperCollins Publishers, 1992), there were two relatively influential Jewish organizations in the U.S. that could have swayed national policy and made a positive difference in the fate of the European Jews.

THE MAIN JEWISH ORGANIZATIONS IN THE UNITED STATES DURING WWII

The first organization, the (non-Zionist) American Jewish Committee, was headed by Cyrus Adler. The second organization, the (Zionist) American Jewish Congress (which expanded into the World Jewish Congress), was headed by Rabbi Stephen Wise. Both could have taken a decisive stance on behalf of their fellow Jews in Europe once they found out that they were faced with annihilation. For the most part, however, they offered only belated, and cautious, support.

More significantly, saving the Jewish populations in Europe was never a priority for the Roosevelt administration, whose efforts focused entirely on winning the war. The fact that the war was a priority for the United States is perfectly understandable. But saving the Jews in Europe, or at least making a concerted effort to help them, would not have significantly impeded the war effort. The policy of both American Jewish organizations and particularly that of the Roosevelt administration—America First—became a determining factor in the decision not to take active steps to help save millions of European Jews from deportation, slave labor, death squads, starvation, and disease in ghettos and concentration camps.

INFORMATION ABOUT THE DEATH CAMPS IN 1942

In 1942, the Allies received reliable information about Hitler's plans to annihilate the Jews throughout Nazi-controlled Europe. This news came from three main sources: Nazi leaders uncomfortable with Hitler's plans to destroy the Jews, Polish officers opposed to the Nazi regime occupying their country, and Jewish escapees or other eyewitnesses. As Hilberg notes in *Perpetrators, Victims, Bystanders*, "during July 1942 . . . several Germans crossed into Switzerland with fundamental revelations. One of them was Ernst Lemmer, a founder of the German Democratic party in 1918 and Minister in West Germany during the 1950's and 1960's. Lemmer . . . met with several Swiss public figures in Zurich that July and told them about 'gas chambers, stationary and mobile, in which Jews were killed'" (236).

Lemmer was not alone. Other reliable sources corroborated this information. Gerhart M. Riegner, the leader of the World Jewish Congress in Geneva (the sister organization of Wise's American Jewish Congress), began collecting this data. He met with the British and American consuls to warn them about Hitler's plans for the annihilation of the European Jews. Gerhart asked the Allied governments to investigate these claims and to inform Rabbi Wise in the United States about them. The government officials didn't deliver this critical information immediately. When Rabbi Wise finally received the news, he and other Jewish leaders set up a meeting with President Roosevelt.

THE MEETING BETWEEN THE U.S. JEWISH LEADERS AND FRANKLIN D. ROOSEVELT

That meeting took place on December 8, 1942. The Jewish delegates were conservative in their estimates. They stated that about 2 million Jews had been killed by death squads and in concentration camps, whereas the actual figure was double. But they were sufficiently alarmed to ask the President to respond, proposing that the United States offer Germany and its allies a warning. They also suggested that the government collect more information about Hitler's plans to kill the Jewish population of Europe by mass shootings, gassing, and other means. By any standard, these were modest requests. Even if implemented, they might not have accomplished much. Roosevelt, Hilberg informs us, "assented to the warning proposal and asked whether the delegates had other recommendations. When the Jewish leaders could not think of anything, Roosevelt switched to other topics" (*Perpetrators, Victims, Bystanders*, 245). Following this meeting, however, the President didn't keep his word. For the most part, the United States did not offer a safe haven for Jewish refugees; it did not bomb the Auschwitz gas chambers (despite doing recognizance flights around Auschwitz and bombing its Monowitz Buna Werke factory); it did not do anything to prevent the deportations and killings of over 400,000 Hungarian Jews as late as 1944, after Germany occupied the country.

The Roosevelt administration, like the American Jewish organizations themselves, did not want to give the impression that the United States was fighting a "mercenary" war on behalf of the European Jews. The noninterventionist efforts of Charles Lindbergh, under the motto "Defend America First," did not succeed in keeping America out of the war after the Japanese attack on Pearl Harbor on December 7, 1941. The next day the United States Congress declared war on Japan. But such nationalist pressures did succeed in encouraging a noninterventionist policy when it came to the tragic fate of the European Jews, many of whom might have been saved were it not for the policy of "America First."

Chapter Twenty-Nine

Quiet Neighbors by Allan A. Ryan

Allan A. Ryan's *Quiet Neighbors* (New York: Harcourt Brace Jovanovich, 1984) depicts some of the horrors that countless Jewish victims lived through in the Nazi death camps. This book also describes the often lengthy and challenging process of bringing the Nazi victimizers and their collaborators to justice. In a little over a year, from July 1942 to August 1943, the Nazis murdered nearly a million Jews at Treblinka. As Ryan recounts,

> The guards drove the dazed and fearful Jews like livestock from the trains to be processed—clothing removed, hair shorn—some snatched out of the streams of people and told to stand aside. Families who had managed to stay together during the suffocating train ride slowly fell apart, their screams, their outstretched arms no match for the disciplined and experienced guards. After their hair was removed, the naked cargo was herded onto a dirt path packed hard by the feet of thousands of people before them. At the end lay gas chambers and, beyond them, deep smoldering pits that sent up thick black smoke to darken the sky. (*Quiet Neighbors*, 2)

Some guards, many of whom were Ukrainian in origin, were particularly cruel and enjoyed torturing their victims before killing them. One of the worst sadists among them was Ivan Marchenko, the man who pumped carbon monoxide into the gas chambers. Known as "Ivan the Terrible" among the prisoners and staff of Treblinka, Ivan was a mountain of a man infamous for beating victims with an iron pipe or cutting off their body parts, just for sport, before he murdered them.

Amazingly, Marchenko, as well as other notorious Nazi collaborators, found refuge in the United States. In fact, Ryan notes, in an ironic twist of fate, it became easier for former Nazi collaborators to immigrate legally to the United States after the war than it was for Holocaust survivors. Ivan changed his name to John Demajanjuk when he came to the United States in 1952. He and his wife moved to Seven Hills, Ohio, where they quietly raised their three kids. By all accounts, the couple was well liked by their neighbors. It took nearly thirty years for the authorities to catch on that Demajanjuk was in actuality Ivan Marchenko, "the Terror of Treblinka," and strip him of his American citizenship.

Ryan argues that the fact that the United States was more likely to harbor the perpetrators than the victims of the Holocaust is not accidental. The U.S. leadership, as we've seen in an earlier chapter, never wanted to give the impression that WWII was fought on behalf of the Jews. Even American Jewish leaders hesitated to apply pressure upon the government, in order to minimize the possibility of provoking a wave of anti-Semitism in the country. In the summer of 1948, President Truman signed the Displaced Persons Act, which allowed 200,000 individuals to immigrate to the United States over a two-year period (16). The vast majority (about 85 percent) of Jewish refugees who wanted to immigrate were excluded from this bill. By way of contrast, immigrants from countries that had collaborated with the Nazis were welcome. "Having excluded nearly all the Jews," Ryan observes, "Congress then extended America's hand to the Balts. It required that 40 percent of the immigrants be from countries that had been "de facto annexed by a foreign power"—a diplomatic euphemism for Latvia, Lithuania, and Estonia, whose incorporation into the Soviet Union in 1944 the United States had never officially recognized" (17). The immigration bill also privileged farmers (offering them 30 percent of the available slots), who formed a high percentage of the non-Jewish Eastern European immigrants and a very low percentage of Jews.

As a *New York Times* journalist aptly summarized the situation, "As matters stand, it is easier for a former Nazi to enter the United States than for one of the Nazi's innocent victims" (19). *Quiet Neighbors* not only follows the extradition trials of some of the most notorious Nazi collaborators who made their way legally into the United States shortly after WWII, but also questions America's topsy-turvy postwar immigration policy, which often privileged perpetrators over victims.

Chapter Thirty

Action T4

From "Euthanasia" to the Final Solution

Since the late fifth century B.C. up to current times, the Hippocratic oath has been taken by doctors to ensure the ethics of the medical profession. Above all, the Hippocratic oath forbids doctors from causing deliberate harm to their patients. Doctors pledge, "I will prescribe regiments for the good of my patients according to my ability and my judgment and never do harm to anyone. I will give no deadly medicine to anyone if asked, nor suggest any such council." The most egregious violation of medical ethics was perpetrated by the Nazi doctors. "Euthanasia," as practiced by Third Reich physicians, set a precedent for the Final Solution. From September 1939 to August 1941, when he faced objections from German religious leaders, Hitler experimented in Germany with Action T4. The program was euphemistically described as "euthanasia." In practice, however, T4 entailed the extermination of individuals in psychiatric institutions deemed "mentally incurable." Over 70,000 patients in mental hospitals were killed under this program. Even when Hitler officially terminated it in 1941, the practice continued until the end of the war.

"T4" is an abbreviation of Tiergarten Street Number 4 in Berlin, the address of the *Charitable Foundation for Curative and Institutional Care* directed by Philipp Bouhler and Karl Brandt, Hitler's personal physician. As Robert Jay Lifton explains in *The Nazi Doctors*, the "euthanasia" program initially employed lethal injection. Later, in order to kill people in greater numbers and more efficiently, Nazi physicians began using carbon monoxide. This method of mass murder was also implemented to kill Jews, Gypsies, and Poles in the concentration camps.

In 1939, Christian Wirth, one of the SS officers in charge of exterminating the Jews of Poland, designed a gas chamber disguised as a public shower. Witnesses describe Wirth as a malicious sadist, similar in psychological profile to Josef Mengele, the notorious "Angel of Death." Corporal Franz Suchomel recalls, "From my activity in the camps of Treblinka and Sobibor, I remember that Wirth in brutality, meanness, and ruthlessness could not be surpassed. We therefore called him 'Christian the Terrible'" (Arad Ytzhak, *Belzec, Sobibor, Treblinka: The Operation Reinhard Death Camps*, p 183–186).

The gas used at first was carbon monoxide, but that proved to be too slow acting. The Nazis then turned to Zyklon B—a cyanide based pesticide—to murder 1.2 million people in the gas chambers. The process, deemed to be a quicker and "more humane" method of killing (compared to mass shootings or carbon monoxide), in actuality caused a slow and excruciating death. In *The Diary of Petr Ginz: 1941–1942*, Chava Pressburger pays homage to her brother Petr, who died in Auschwitz at the age of sixteen. She is particularly pained by the thought that her brother died such an agonizing death:

> I ask readers to forgive me for returning to that terrible description. The witness in question worked in the gas chambers. His task was to wait for the people shoved into the gas chamber to suffocate; then he had to open the chamber and transport the heaps of corpses to the ovens, where they were to be burned. This man could barely speak for tears. He testified that the position of corpses suggested what went on inside the hermetically sealed chamber, when it began to be filled with toxic gas. The stronger ones, led by an overpowering instinct for self-preservation, tried to get to the top, where there was still some air left, so that the weaker ones were trampled to death. (131)

Conceptually, the distance between the Action T4 program implemented in German mental hospitals and the mass murder in concentration camps was small. The T4 program offered the framework for the Final Solution. As Allan Bullock observes in *Hitler and Stalin: Parallel Lives*, Action T4 set the following precedents for mass extermination:

1. It established an atmosphere of secrecy, shrouded in a language filled with codes and euphemisms to describe torture and murder.

2. It implicated doctors in murder through a procedural façade of medical professionalism (including physical examinations, diagnoses, and the administration of "medicines" or "operations").

3. From the very beginning, it set Jewish patients apart from others for "special treatment." Jews did not have to meet the T4 criteria—namely, of being diagnosed with incurable diseases or mental disorders—in

order to be killed. They could be killed simply because they were Jewish (*Hitler and Stalin*, 746).

Perhaps the most valuable lesson Hitler drew from the T4 program was to move the killing machine outside his own country. Following vocal protests by the Protestant pastors Paul-Gerhard Braune and Fritz von Bodelschwingh and by Cardinal August Count von Galen, Hitler decided to bide his time and kill more covertly—not in Germany, where he wished to remain popular, but in the conquered territories, where he would have free reign. The opportunity presented itself when he attacked Russia in Operation Barbarossa on June 22, 1941. With the onset of war, all bets were off. The Nazis used the fight against "the Bolshevik empire" as a justification for putting into practice everything they had learned from the Action T4 "euthanasia" program.

Chapter Thirty-One

Hitler's Niece and Historical Fiction

If you want to learn about Hitler's life, read Ian Kershaw's *Hitler: A Biography* (W. W. Norton & Company, 2010). If you want to find out about the history of the Nazi movement and Hitler's role in it, read *Hitler and Stalin: Parallel Lives* by Alan Bullock (Knopf, 1992). But if you want to get a sense of who Hitler was as a human being, I would encourage you to read Ron Hansen's historical fiction, *Hitler's Niece* (Harper Collins, 1999). The novel traces Hitler's abnormal psychology from the perspective of Angela Maria ("Geli") Raubal (1908–1931), his half niece. Geli is intelligent, beautiful, full of joie de vivre and untouched by the political obsessions and anti-Semitic hatred of her powerful uncle and his entourage. She maintains an ironic distance from Hitler's fanatical followers—Rudolf Hess, Heinrich Himmler, Joseph Goebbels, Hermann Göring, and Alfred Rosenberg—who also appear in the novel. Compared to her, however, they're wooden characters in a farce. These vain men are fawning and obsequious, hungry for power, and ready to not merely follow, but also anticipate Hitler's wishes.

By the author's own admission, the novel doesn't adhere strictly to historical facts. It is only inspired by them, particularly by Bullock's political biography *Hitler and Stalin*, which Hansen states provoked his fascination with Geli Raubal (Author's Note, 307–308). The novel describes her life from beginning to end; from birth to tragic death. We find out that Geli's father died at the age of 31, leaving her mother, Angela, to take care of three kids (Geli, Leo, and Elfriede) with practically no source of income. After seeing that Geli, at seventeen, had bloomed into a lovely young woman, Hitler invited his niece to be his housekeeper and companion. Her mother gladly accepted this rather unorthodox arrangement in the hopes of making possible a better lifestyle for their family. Becoming Hitler's companion, caretaker, maid, and eventually his (ambiguous) mistress, Geli catches a glimpse of the inner workings of the Nazi party. Above all, *Hitler's Niece* shows us, up close and personal, how a psychopath capable of genocide "falls in love." Even after her death, Hitler considered Geli the love of his life. Neither Eva Braun, his doting life companion, nor any other woman could compete with his obsession with his niece.

Geli Raubal spent six years either living with Hitler or being in frequent contact with him. For a period of time, she lived in his Munich apartment while she studied medicine and took music lessons. She also accompanied him to the opera, cinema, and some of the other social functions he attended. The plot of the novel hinges on their sexual tension as well as on Geli's psychological trauma as she becomes, increasingly against her will, Hitler's sexual partner in a sordid, sadomasochistic relationship that sickens her and intoxicates him. The more she tries to escape him, the more clingy and desperate Hitler becomes. As the narrator states, "She was his escape, his torpor, his surrender to the vacillation and passivity that were increasingly part of his nature" (220).

Dependency and obsessive desire, however, don't equal love. For love to exist, the lover has to be able to consider, empathize with and fulfill the beloved's own needs as a separate individual. Hitler can't do that. His idea of interesting conversation is bragging incessantly about himself. His idea of affection is engaging in perverse and demeaning sexual rituals. His idea of respect reveals his fundamental misogyny. His idea of passion is possession and control of the object of his desire. Hitler demands to know at all times where Geli is, what she is doing and with whom. He retains the freedom to see other mistresses, including Eva Braun, but keeps Geli on a tight leash, discouraging any potential suitors. Once Emil Maurice, Hitler's good-looking Corsican chauffeur, begins dating Geli, Hitler finds a pretext to dismiss him. "She is with *me*," he later snarls when another man, Schirach, asks his permission to take out Geli on a date (244).

Feeling trapped by her uncle's overpowering addiction to her, Geli cannot escape the misery that dominates her life. When she expresses her distress, her friends turn their backs on her. Even her mother essentially prostitutes her to "Uncle Alf," "the patriarch of the family," rather than face poverty again. *Hitler's Niece* also adds an interesting, but largely speculative, twist to the story of Geli's life. Although the official version of her biography states that Geli committed suicide in 1931, in the novel, Hitler, realizing that he can no longer control his niece, beats her, breaks her nose and then shoots her. His entourage quickly covers up the murder and presents it to the police and the media as a suicide. This adds an intriguing element of mystery to the plot, turning *Hitler's Niece* into a detective story. But the novel's main strength remains the psychological aspect of the drama. Hansen helps us see that, in terms of lacking empathy and a conscience, there is not much difference between Hitler the public man, who could order the murder of millions of innocent people, and Hitler the private lover, who prefers to destroy the object of his desire rather than risk losing her. In both cases, Hitler is a remorseless killer.

Given this novel's many strengths, it's surprising to me that *Hitler's Niece* received some scathing reviews, particularly from *The New York Times*. In his review "Springtime for Hitler, in love with his niece," Michiko Kakutani offers a plot summary and then dismisses the novel as a poor representation of history, which takes away from the gruesome reality of Hitler's "public crimes, crimes that tragically were not speculative imaginings of a novelist, crimes that have been consigned to the margins of this inept and voyeuristic novel" (NYT, September 7, 1999).

I disagree with Kakutani's harsh assessment of the novel and standards of evaluation. The role of historical fiction is not to convey history accurately or in great detail. That is what (nonfiction) history books do. In my opinion, the role of historical fiction is to do exactly what *Hitler's Niece* does quite well: namely, to find inspiration in real historical events and to imagine the mindset, emotions and desires of its key figures. Often only more marginal characters, such as Geli Raubal, Hitler's niece, can give us a three-dimensional picture of the monster whose acts have marred the pages of history.

Chapter Thirty-Two

An Unlikely Hero

Schindler's List by Thomas Keneally

Slavery is the most debasing system of labor in human civilization, reducing people to the status of property. Slaves are bought and sold like objects. They are forced to work for free or for flimsy compensation, usually in grueling and inhumane conditions. Sometimes they are raped, beaten, or killed by their owners. They are, by definition, deprived of human rights and dignity. With the exception of the Holocaust, I can't think of any other period in history when slaves desired slavery and when forced labor became a saving grace for the exploited workers. Yet in such a dark epoch, when everything conspired to wipe the Jewish people off the face of the Earth, enslaving over a thousand of them in an enamel factory became an act of courage.

As incredible as this topsy-turvy perspective may seem to contemporary readers, this is the story of Thomas Keneally's famous novel, *Schindler's List*. The novel is based on the eyewitness accounts provided by several of the Jewish survivors saved during the Holocaust by the German industrialist Oskar Schindler. This is a biographical novel in the strict sense of the term. As Keneally states, "most exchanges and conversations, and all events, are based on the detailed recollections of the *Schindlerjuden* (Schindler Jews), of Schindler himself, and of other witnesses to Oskar's acts of outrageous rescue" (New York: Touchstone, *Schindler's List*, 1982, Author's Note, 10).

Oskar Schindler is, by the author's own account, an unlikely hero. As Keneally acknowledges in the Prologue, Schindler "was not a virtuous man in the customary sense of the term" (*Schindler's List*, 14). We tend to think of heroes as people of extraordinary character and moral fortitude. Yet Oskar Schindler was an average man with ordinary human foibles. He was a sensualist and a womanizer. He openly cheated on his wife, Emilie, with long-term mistresses and casual lovers. He enjoyed carousing with his friends, business partners, acquaintances and escorts. Moreover, he was a member of the Nazi party, initially joining its ranks out of genuine political conviction.

Though quickly disillusioned with the Nazis, Schindler nonetheless hopes to profit financially from their regime. An ethnic German from the Sudetenland, he moves to Krakow, Poland to set up an enamelware factory that relies upon the slave labor of the local Jews. The large Jewish community in Krakow was isolated from the rest of the population by the Nazis in a Jewish Ghetto, which was established in March 1941 in the Podgorze district. Schindler witnesses the cruelty manifested by the SS towards the 15,000 helpless Jewish civilians as well as the random acts of violence of his sociopathic acquaintance, Amos Goeth, who regards the captive Jews as his prey and property.

This biographical novel presents a slice of history and a study of contrasts between times of normalcy and the mass insanity of the Nazi era and between the humane actions of Oskar Schindler and the savage inhumanity of Amon Goeth. Without the dark figure of Goeth serving as a foil to the protagonist, it would be more difficult to appreciate Schindler's humanity.

Amos Goeth, the SS Second Lieutenant in charge of liquidating the Krakow Ghetto and of overseeing the Plaszow concentration and labor camp, is a malicious sadist. He savagely beats his Jewish servant, Helen Hirsch, and kills Jewish inmates, randomly, just for sport. As the narrator states, "No one knew Amon's precise reason for settling on that prisoner—Amon certainly did not have to document his motives. With one blast from the doorstep, the man was plucked from the group of pushing and pulling captives and hurled sideways in the road" (192).

By way of contrast to Goeth's vicious cat and mouse games, Schindler exhibits courage and compassion. He uses his connections, resourcefulness and wealth to save the lives of as many Jews as possible. Threatened by the advance of the Russian army on the Eastern front, the Nazis dismantle the Plaszow labor and concentration camp. When he finds out about their plans to send most of the prisoners to Auschwitz, Schindler promises those who work for him that he would save their lives. He sets up a small munitions factory in his hometown of Brinnlitz, Czechoslovakia, where he eventually manages to bring over 1,500 Jews. In these horrific times, slavery becomes the Jews' only hope of salvation. "Oskar's list, in the mind of some, was already more than a mere fabulation. It was a *List*. It was a sweet chariot which might swing low" (277).

The Fascist regimes brought out the worst in many people throughout Germany and occupied Europe: at best, a cruel indifference to the enslavement and massacre of the Jews; at worst, various degrees of collusion with the killers. Yet these dark times also brought out the best in a few individuals, such as Oskar Schindler. His courage and resourcefulness have inspired the blockbuster movie, *Schindler's List* (1993), directed by Steven Spielberg. But the greatest homage to this ordinary man who did his best to protect fellow human beings from the Nazi savagery remains that he will be remembered and honored by generations of Jews as an extraordinary hero.

Chapter Thirty-Three

The Boy in the Striped Pajamas

An Instructive Fable

The Boy in the Striped Pajamas, the controversial bestselling novel by John Boyne, is described in its subtitle as a "fable." The novel doesn't propose to offer a realistic historical account of the Holocaust. A fable, by definition, uses make-believe characters and circumstances to convey a simple moral lesson. This novel is relatively short, only 216 pages. Boyne claimed that he wrote it all in one fell swoop, in two and a half days. Written simply, from the perspective of a German nine-year-old boy whose father is in charge of the Auschwitz concentration camp, this novel is commonly taught, along with *The Diary of Anne Frank*, in U.S. middle schools and high schools to introduce students to the Holocaust.

The Boy in the Striped Pajamas (New York: Random House, 2006) fared well worldwide, selling over 5 million copies and becoming a bestseller in Ireland, the United Kingdom, Spain and Australia. The novel achieved such popularity that it was made into a film in 2008 directed by Mark Herman, starring Asa Butterfield, Jack Scanlon, David Thewlis, Vera Farmiga, Amber Beattie, and Ruper Friend. Although widely acclaimed, *The Boy in the Striped Pajamas* has also been harshly criticized. Rabbi Benjamin Blech called it "not just a lie and not just a fairytale, but a profanation." He's not alone in arguing that the novel paints a distorted image of life in the Nazi concentration camps.

The novel is, admittedly, unrealistic. It describes the encounter between Bruno, the privileged nine-year-old son of a prominent Nazi party leader, and Shmuel, a downtrodden young prisoner in Auschwitz who has the same birthday and age as Bruno. The two meet nearly every day and talk for hours, for about a year, across the fence of the concentration camp. In real life, even one such encounter would have been highly improbable. A meeting between a prisoner and the Nazi officer's son lasting hours, day after day, would have been impossible. Auschwitz was closely monitored by vigilant soldiers with weapons, guarded by attack dogs and surrounded by an electric fence. Moreover, Jewish prisoners observed a strict regimen, which involved slave labor and early morning roll calls that would take hours and forced marches that were sheer torture. Generally speaking, children under the age of fifteen were immediately selected for extermination as soon as they arrived at Auschwitz. No Jewish nine-year-old could have been absent for hours a day to chat amicably with a German boy, much less the son of a prominent Nazi officer. Moreover, if even one such conversation could have taken place, presumably it would have quickly dispelled Bruno's ignorance about how Jewish children and their parents were treated at Auschwitz. The German boy would have ceased to wonder why Shmuel was so thin and why he was always hungry.

Nevertheless, in assessing the merits of this novel, we need to keep in mind that *The Boy in the Striped Pajamas* is not presented as either fact or historical fiction. It is a fable. The main literary technique it uses in adopting the more or less innocent, if privileged, perspective of Bruno, is what the Russian formalist critic, Mikhail Bakhtin, called "ostranenie" or "defamiliarization." Bruno's innocent perspective exposes the assumptions of the grownups he deals with: his father, the Nazi leader; his mother, who is apolitical but nonetheless a beneficiary of the system; the servants who are afraid to speak their minds; and even his older sister, twelve-year-old Gretel, who has already begun to accept the prejudices of the adults around her. Only Bruno can't understand why his new friend, Shmuel, is skeletal, why he must wear striped pajamas every day, why the Jews are mistreated in this fashion, or why he, himself, has to live isolated from his peers in a big house near Auschwitz. Though quite bright, and more thoughtful and curious than the adults around him, Bruno acts younger than his years. His childlike innocence corresponds to the perspective of a six or seven-year-old boy.

As historical fact, the novel would be off the mark. As a fable, however, *The Boy in the Striped Pajamas* delivers a worthwhile message. It shows how even loving parents can corrupt their children into believing that other religions, ethnicities, or races are subhuman or inferior to theirs. It reveals the social conditioning, which begins at home, that normalizes class and racial hierarchies as well as prejudice, violence, and hatred against the Jews (or any other social groups). These perspectives are so counterintuitive to Bruno that he willingly steps into Shmuel's shoes—or, in this case, leaves his behind—in order to help his friend find his lost father in the concentration camp. As one can imagine, this decision has dire consequences.

Though far removed from the stark realism of Holocaust memoirs as well as from the objectivity of well-documented histories, *The Boy in the Striped*

Pajamas is nevertheless a successful thought experiment. This fable invites readers to envision what it must feel like to learn prejudice and racism from a very young age in a culture that divides people in terms of the binary categories of human and subhuman.

Chapter Thirty-Four

Forgiven but Never Forgotten

There is a powerful phrase among those sympathetic to Holocaust victims and survivors: Never again! This phrase has two meanings. In one sense, it refers to the sufferings of the Jewish people: Never again allow another Holocaust against *the Jews*. In another sense, it expresses a universal message for humanity: Never again allow another genocide based upon discrimination and hatred of *any* group of people. I interpret the phrase "Never again!" in the second, broader sense, which I believe is more meaningful. Although the Holocaust was certainly about the massacre of Jews as Jews, obviously the genocide of any group of people is ethically wrong. In this second sense of the phrase "Never again," the incarceration, starvation, torture, and killings of American prisoners of war during WWII by the Japanese belongs side by side to the history of the Holocaust.

Remarkably, American prisoners of war captured by the Nazis fared better than those captured by the Japanese. Although they killed ten million innocent people in concentration camps and via shooting squads throughout Europe, the Nazis were careful in their conduct towards non-Jewish Allied prisoners of war. Generally speaking, Allied POWs lived in better conditions than Jewish, Polish, Russian and Ukrainian prisoners and consequently had better chances of survival.

By way of contrast, American POWs were in extreme danger when captured by the Japanese. They were subjected to similar mistreatment and conditions that Jewish prisoners had to endure at the hands of the Nazis: starvation, filth, disease, physical, and psychological torture, slave labor and death. Of the 132,000 POWs from the United States, Great Britain, New Zealand, Australia, and Holland forced into concentration and labor camps in Japan, more than a quarter of them—and about 40 percent of Americans—died in captivity. By way of contrast, only one percent of American POWs held by the Nazis died in captivity (*Unbroken*, Laura Hillenbrand, New York: Random House, 2010, 314–315).

Although the Japanese didn't have crematoria like the Nazis, they adopted a "kill all" approach to American POWs during WWII. Their policy was also inherently racist. The Japanese attitude towards foreigners was informed by xenophobia and a sense of ethnic supremacy not only vis-à-vis the Americans, but also towards their Chinese, Korean, and European captives. There are striking similarities between the racist outlook and behavior of the Japanese under the Prime Minister Hideki Tojo and that of the Germans under Adolf Hitler, his ally.

It's therefore not all that surprising that the remarkable memoir of resilience and survival, *Unbroken*, a *New York Times* best seller that has been made into a major motion picture directed by Angelina Jolie, reads like a Holocaust memoir. Beautifully narrated by Laura Hillenbrand, *Unbroken* tells the life story of Louis Zamperini, a young soldier and star runner of the Berlin Olympics, who defies the odds in his struggle to survive war and captivity.

On May 1943, Zamperini's plane crashes into the Pacific Ocean. There are only three survivors: Louis and two of his friends. Together they embark on an Odyssean voyage across the world. They're stranded on a raft without food or water, drifting for thousands of miles, threatened by inclement weather and assailed by sharks. They catch fish using bird meat as bait and collect rainwater to quench their thirst. They patch up the raft when enemy bullets pierce it and fight off sharks with their bare hands. Weakened by starvation, thirst, exhaustion and depression, one of them, Francis McNamara (Mac), gives up the fight for survival and perishes before they reach land. The other two men, Louis Zamperini and Russell Allen Phillips (Phil), brave a typhoon and make it to a distant island. The most difficult and dangerous part of their journey, however, consists of attacks by fellow human beings.

The young men are captured by the Japanese, then incarcerated, interrogated and sent to concentration camps for POWs. Louis is first sent to Ofunaand and later to Naoetsu. In both camps, the conditions are inhumane. The goal of their captors is total human degradation. Louis recalls two particularly sadistic guards who got a thrill out of attacking and torturing prisoners: Sueharu Kitamura, known as "the Quack," who beat Louis's friend, the brilliant Bill Harris, to unconsciousness, and Corporal Mutsuhiro Watanabe, dubbed "the Bird," a vicious psychopath. "The Bird" relishes tormenting Louis in particular, partly because he's a "prize"—a star American athlete. Alternating between savage beatings and disingenuous shows of compassion, this monster becomes the bane of Louis's existence, haunting him long after he's freed from captivity.

Much of Louis Zamperini's post-traumatic stress disorder after liberation takes the form of nightmares in which he envisions strangling his former tormentor. This imaginary resolution doesn't relieve his pain, however. As the narrator reflects, "The paradox of vengefulness is that it makes men dependent upon those who have harmed them, believing that their release from pain will come only when they make their tormentors suffer. In seeking the Bird's death to free himself, Louie had chained himself, once again, to his tyrant" (*Unbroken*, 366).

Although welcomed home as a hero, Louis can't escape the trauma of his war experiences. He drowns his bitter memories with alcohol and sinks into a deep depression. Fortunately, religion as well as his supportive and loving family eventually help him overcome this last challenge. Louis's greatest strength, however, stems from his resilience: the capacity to forgive his tormentors without forgetting his painful past. One of the most compelling messages of his incredible life story is: let go of the pain, so you can move on, but not of the memories that make up your identity. This lesson applies to both individuals and groups. "Never again!" means, in this case, forgive the enemy but never forget the experience, so that you can impart your wisdom to future generations.

Chapter Thirty-Five

The 1936 Berlin Olympics

The Boys in the Boat

In 1936, Hitler held the Summer Olympics in Berlin. He spared no expense to impress the world with the prowess and superiority of Nazi Germany. He built six gymnasiums, numerous arenas and an enormous track and field stadium with a capacity of 100,000 seats. He also commissioned his favorite filmmaker, Leni Riefenstahl, to create a documentary called *Olympia* about the event, which focused on the prowess of the German athletes. This groundbreaking film employed several new techniques that would become the staple of documentaries about athletic events: including extreme close-ups, smash cuts (abrupt changes of scenes without transition), and unusual camera angles that captured the viewers' attention. *Olympia* received high praise, internationally.

Daniel James Brown's novel *The Boys in the Boat: Nine Americans and Their Epic Quest for Gold at the 1936 Berlin Olympics* (New York: Penguin Books, 2014) relates this historic event from an American perspective. The book focuses in particular on the point of view of Joe Rantz, a poor boy from Seattle abandoned by his father and stepmother at a very young age, who is left to fend for himself. Brown's prose, reminiscent of another bestseller about this era—Laura Hillenbrand's *Unbroken*—describes Joe's problems with his family, his long-lasting love for Joyce, his loyal teenage sweetheart, and the arduous practice sessions with his teammates in preparation for the Olympics. Offering an engaging perspective on the sport of rowing and a slice of life about the Great Depression, *The Boys in the Boat* also depicts the moment in European history when the Nazi regime consolidated power and gained international recognition.

By 1936, Hitler had already instituted the Nuremberg Race Laws in Germany. In 1935, at the annual Nazi party rally held in Nuremberg, the Fuhrer announced laws that defined the racial concept of a "Jew" and a "half-Jew," excluded German Jews from citizenship and prohibited them from marrying or having sexual relations with Aryans. He also imposed numerous economic sanctions upon German Jews. The implications of the Nuremberg Laws extended to the 1936 Olympics. Hitler planned to ban Jews and African Americans from the Olympic games. The official Nazi newspaper, the *Volkischer Beobachter*, declared that these groups should not be allowed to participate in the Olympics in Berlin. Once several nations objected to such racism and threatened to boycott the event, however, Hitler momentarily relented. He abandoned the racial prohibitions and even allowed a half-Jewish German woman, Helene Mayer, to participate on the German team. He also ordered the temporary removal of conspicuous discriminatory signs such as "Jews not wanted" from the streets of Berlin.

The Boys in the Boat delves into Nazi history and propaganda, even capturing the mutual attraction—as well as the tension and competition for Hitler's favor—between the filmmaker Leni Riefenstahl and Joseph Goebbels, the Nazi Minister of Public Enlightenment and Propaganda. Notorious for his voracious sexual appetite and affairs with young movie stars, Goebbels tries to seduce Riefenstahl following their flirtatious interactions. In several dramatically described episodes, Riefenstahl rejects his advances and even complains to Hitler about Goebbels' interference into her filming of the Olympics. Nonetheless, the author makes it clear that the talented filmmaker and the lecherous Minister of Propaganda share a common goal. Like Hitler, they want to see the triumph of the German athletes.

Their desires are frustrated by the unexpected victory of the underdogs. The American team wins against all odds, despite the fact that two of their rowers fell ill before the race, the home crowd cheered for Germany, and they were given the worst lane. Italy wins second place and Germany comes in third. In some respects, the narrative conveys the American athletic victory not only as the personal triumph of Joe Rantz and his teammates, but also as a partial victory over Nazism. In the end, Hitler leaves the balcony, furious over his country's defeat. Thus *The Boys in the Boat* transforms an important athletic event into a memorable part of world history.

Chapter Thirty-Six

Manufacturing Death

Hell's Cartel

IG Farben didn't start out as a Nazi death factory, which is what it's known for to this day. In fact, up to the mid-1930s, its chief executives were not even particularly anti-Semitic. Formed in 1925, IG Farben began as a chemical company that manufactured dye. The business was so successful that by the 1930s it became the largest chemical company in the world and the fourth largest company in general. One of its directors, Carl Bosch, was awarded the Nobel Prize in Chemistry in 1931 for the development of chemical high-pressure methods. In *Hell's Cartel: IG Farben and the Making of Hitler's War Machine* (New York, Henry Holt and Company, 2008), Diarmuid Jeffreys describes the progression—or rather, the regression—of IG Farben from Germany's leading chemical company to a death factory during the Holocaust.

Jeffreys records one of the most telling moments of this transition: the episode when the company's leader, Carl Bosch, who valued the scientific work of many of his Jewish colleagues and employees, paid a visit to Hitler in the attempt to change his anti-Semitic outlook by pointing out its negative impact on science. Predictably, the Fuhrer not only didn't budge, but also refused to communicate with Bosch henceforth:

> Then Bosch, as delicately as he could, raised the "Jewish question." Perhaps the Fuhrer didn't realize the potentially damaging consequences of his policies, he suggested. If more and more Jewish scientists were forced abroad, German physics and chemistry could be set back a hundred years. To his alarm, Hitler erupted in fury. Obviously the businessman knew nothing of politics, he snarled. If necessary, Germany would "work one hundred years

without physics and chemistry." Bosch tried to continue but Hitler rang for an aide and told him icily, "The Geheimrat wishes to leave." (*Hell's Cartel*, 178)

When the company's senior executives Carl Bosch and Carl Duisberg retired, they were replaced by a new crop of leaders who toed the party line. The company started to follow a more "pragmatic" approach, catering to the gruesome needs of the Nazi regime. By 1941, IG Farben became directly involved in the death machine at Auschwitz. It built a rubber factory called Monowitz, or Auschwitz III, monitored by IG Farben managers and run through the exploitation of slave labor. Prisoners were worked to death there in identical conditions to the rest of the concentration camp. They were fed the same insufficient food, were guarded by the same brutal SS prisoners, lacked health care, and were subject to the same reprisals and torture as the rest of the prisoners at the Auschwitz complex. Most inmates could only survive two to three months working in such harsh conditions. When they were no longer fit for work, they were sent to the gas chamber.

After the war, observing the precedent set by the Nuremberg Trial, some of the leaders of IG Farben were indicted before a U.S. Tribunal led by General Telford Taylor. In 1947 and 1948, twenty-four defendants faced similar charges to those leveled a few years earlier against the Nazi war criminals:

1. Planning and waging a war of aggression against other countries
2. War crimes and crimes against humanity through destroying occupied territories
3. War crimes against humanity through the enslavement, deportation, rape, torture and murder of civilians
4. Membership in the SS, a criminal organization
5. Conspiring to commit the crimes outlined above

In the end, as General Taylor would remark with great disappointment after the trial, justice was not served. Only thirteen of the company's senior executives received prison terms, and even in those cases, only one to eight years (*Hell's Cartel*, 400). The rest of those indicted were released. Several of them became successful executives in other companies. After the war, IG Farben was fractured but not destroyed. The Soviet Union took over part of it. The Western branch of the company continued to thrive, eventually becoming affiliated with Standard Oil. Because of its association with the Holocaust, the remnants of the company faced continual public protests. Although IG Farben executives announced in 2001 that the company would be dissolved by 2003, it continues to exist today, still in the process of liquidation.

Chapter Thirty-Seven

Prosecuting War Crimes

The Nuremberg Trial

How do you punish the perpetrators of the biggest genocide in human history? Do they deserve a fair trial, which their millions of victims never got? These are two of the important questions debated by the Allies during and following WWII. They were eventually resolved at the Nuremberg Trial, which Ann and John Tusa describe in their book by the same name (*The Nuremberg Trial*, New York: Atheneum, 1986). Several options were suggested, even before the war was over and the Ally victory secured. Documents released in 2006 from the British War Cabinet indicate that in December 1944 the Cabinet considered a swift and severe punishment of the Nazi officials involved in crimes against humanity.

Winston Churchill suggested the summary execution of the top Nazi leaders. A year earlier, at the Tehran Conference, Joseph Stalin proposed executing 50,000 to 100,000 Nazi officers. Roosevelt appeared prepared to go on board with this idea, but Churchill objected, stating that most of these officers were fighting for their country. Roosevelt later considered a plan proposed by the US Secretary of Treasury, Henry Morgenthau. Morgenthau called for the de-industrialization of Germany and the execution of the major Nazi war criminals. This proposed retribution, once publicized by the media, provoked popular protests in the United States, which dissuaded Roosevelt from pursuing it.

The plan eventually adopted by President Harry S. Truman after Roosevelt's death continues to serve as a precedent and role model for prosecuting war crimes. The trial that took place in 1945 and 1946 in the city of Nuremberg sharply distinguishes itself from how totalitarian regimes had administered "justice" by leveling false accusations against millions of innocent people and murdering them.

The Allies chose Nuremberg for the trial of the top Nazi leaders for several reasons:

1. Its Palace of Justice was one of the few public buildings in major cities in Germany that had withstood the Ally bombings and remained relatively intact.
2. The building included a large prison.
3. Nuremberg was the ceremonial place where the Nazis held rallies and issued their infamous anti-Semitic legislature.

The International Military Tribunal tried twenty-four Nazi perpetrators for *crimes against peace* (planning and waging wars of aggression), *war crimes* (violations of internationally agreed upon rules of waging war), and *crimes against humanity* (murder, extermination, enslavement, rape and deportation of civilians). Needless to say, not all of the leading perpetrators of Nazi atrocities were caught and punished. Hitler, along with Goebbels and his family had already committed suicide. Many Nazi war criminals, including Adolf Eichmann, scattered throughout the world and lived, for several years, in hiding. Others, such as Heinrich Himmler, disguised themselves as ordinary soldiers in the numerous camps throughout Europe. As the Tusas point out, it was very difficult to catch these mass murderers:

> Given the vast number of such camps, not just in the Four Zones of Germany but in Austria and the liberated countries, all of which were constantly receiving new inmates, checking them was time consuming and frustrating. There was too little communication between the searchers and the authorities who might hold their prey; up-to-date intelligence circulated haphazardly if at all. Under these circumstances it is hardly surprising that the roundup of many leading Nazi war criminals took months. (*The Nuremberg Trial*, 37)

It's remarkable that, despite massive post-war mass migrations and chaos, twenty-four of the leading Nazi war criminals were found and stood trial in Nuremberg. They included Hermann Goering (Hitler's heir), Joachim von Ribbentrop (Nazi Foreign Minister), Rudolf Hess (Hitler's deputy), Hans Frank (the ruthless Governor-General of occupied Poland), Wilhelm Keitel (Army Head), Wilhelm Frick (Minister of Interior), Erns Kaltenbrunner (Security Chief), Konstantin von Neurath (Governor of Moravia and Bohemia), Erich Raeder (Navy Chief), Karl Doenitz (Raeder's successor), Alfred Jodl (Commander of Armed Forces), Alfred Rosenberg (the blood-thristy Minister for the Occupied Eastern Territories), Baldur von Fritz Sauckel (Chief of Forced Labor), Albert Speer (Armaments Minister), Baldur von Schirach

(Hitler Youth Leader), Julius Streicher (leading writer of anti-Semitic propaganda), Alfred Seyss-Inquart (the ingratiating Commissioner for the Occupied Netherlands), and Martin Bormann (Hitler's Adjunct, who was tried in his absence).

Despite their positions of leadership and direct communications with Hitler and Himmler, most of the accused claimed ignorance of the Holocaust. When faced with irrefutable evidence of their involvement in mass murder, they argued that they were merely following orders and serving their country. Most of them adopted an obsequious demeanor in court. The Tusas note two exceptions: Goering and Speer. Hermann Goering behaved in a characteristically bombastic manner. During the trial, he acted in control of the situation. After being sentenced to death, he committed suicide in his cell rather than relinquish power. Albert Speer, the Minister of Defense, made some powerful arguments and was sentenced to only twenty years in prison despite his key role in the Nazi regime. Robert H. Jackson, the United States prosecutor, shone throughout the trial in his eloquence, fairness and passion.

On October 1, 1946, the International Military Tribunal issued the verdicts. Twelve of the most notorious war criminals, including Goering, Ribbentrop, Rosenberg, Frank and Seyss-Inquart, received the death penalty. Three of the accused (Hess, Funk and Raeder) were sentenced to life in prison. Four men (Doenitz, Schirach, Speer and Neurath) received jail terms ranging from 10 to 20 years.

The Nuremberg trial has been described as "the greatest trial in history." During the proceedings, the Allies showed incredible restraint, given the immeasurable harm caused by the Nazis. The trial could have staged a farce of justice, giving the war criminals a taste of their own medicine. But it didn't. The Allies took the high road instead. This is one of the main reasons why the Nuremberg trial continues to serve as a role model for how to deal with war crimes in as fair a fashion as possible, despite the understandable temptation for retribution and revenge.

Chapter Thirty-Eight

Kamikaze Warfare

Inferno

Japan's *kamikaze* pilots during WWII call to mind the operations of contemporary suicide bombers and terrorists. Heavily indoctrinated during their training in the Japanese Imperial army, their suicidal missions did serious damage to the Allied naval vessels in the Pacific, particularly toward the end of the war, in 1944–1945, when Japan's military situation became desperate. Captain Motoharu Okamura, who led the Tateyama Base in Tokyo and the 341's Air Group Base, was one of the first to propose kamikaze warfare, in June 1944, and to explore its feasibility. In October 1944, Commander Asaiki Tamai led an actual mission comprised of twenty-four student pilots whom he had personally trained.

Named after the fatal typhoons of the late Middle Ages ("kami," meaning "god," or "spirit" and kaze," meaning "wind"), these suicidal pilots would direct their whirling airplanes filled with explosives and fuel into enemy vessels, doing more damage than conventional bombs. Launching themselves with fatal accuracy, according to historian Max Hastings, "about 20 percent of kamikaze assaults scored hits—ten times the success rate of conventional attacks. Only the overwhelming strength of the U.S. Navy enabled it to withstand such punishment" (*Inferno, the World at War 1939–1945*, New York: Random House, 2012). During WWII, nearly 4,000 kamikaze pilots died. The damage they inflicted upon the Allies was extensive: the U.S. Air Force webpage indicates that about 3,000 kamikaze attackers sunk thirty-four ships and killed about 5,000 sailors. All in all, about 10 percent of ships hit by kamikaze pilots sank.

What drove these impetuous bombers to sacrifice their lives for the Japanese Empire? Were their suicide missions coerced or voluntary? According to Hastings, most kamikaze pilots went to their final battles willingly, but some were coerced or peer-pressured into acquiescing. Psychological indoctrination played a big role in the Japanese military system, where training was meant to induce unquestioning patriotism, self-sacrifice for the Japanese Empire and a code of honor that prescribed suicide over being captured by the enemy. Hastings emphasizes that the training of the kamikaze pilots "was as harsh as that of all Japanese warriors, and attended by the same emphasis on corporal punishment" that would make them ruthless, and often very cruel, warriors (620). Even so, as it became increasingly clear that Japan would lose the war, not all kamikaze pilots went willingly to their deaths. According to Hastings,

> The image of Japan's kamikazes taking off to face death with exuberant enthusiasm is largely fallacious. Among the first wave of suicidalists in the autumn of 1944, there were many genuine volunteers. Thereafter, however, the supply of young fanatics dwindled: many subsequent recruits were driven to accept the role by moral pressure, and sometimes conscription. (620)

As is the case with contemporary suicide bombers, heavy ideological indoctrination, and a Manichean view of the world—a good versus evil, us versus them mentality—drove the kamikaze bombers to their dark and desperate heroism.

Chapter Thirty-Nine

Hateful Words

Nazi Propaganda

The freedom of expression can be a double-edged sword. Without it, no other freedom is possible. Yet this freedom can also lead to the consolidation of totalitarian regimes when groups defined by hatred and discrimination use it to further their political goals. This is exactly what happened with the rise of the Nazi regime. The freedom of expression, which was more or less respected by the Weimar Republic, was turned into propaganda: hateful words and grandiose nationalist promises used to sway the public to support Nazi ideology.

An inherently manipulative man, Adolf Hitler realized from the start the value of propaganda. His autobiographical treatise *Mein Kampf* (1926) includes three chapters on the importance of propaganda in shaping public opinion. Hitler states, "Propaganda must always address itself to the broad masses of the people. . . . The art of propaganda consists precisely in being able to awaken the imagination of the public through an appeal to their feelings." He continues to argue that these feelings can, and should, be biased as opposed to aiming for the truth: "Propaganda must not investigate the truth objectively and, in so far as it is favorable to the other side, present it to the theoretical rules of justice; yet it must present only that aspect of the truth which is favorable to its own side" (*Mein Kampf*, translated by Ralph Manheim, New York: Houghton Mifflin, 1998).

Once the Nazis rose to power in 1933, Hitler promptly set up a Reich Ministry of Propaganda under the leadership of Joseph Goebbels. The propaganda machine took over all forms of expression including art, film, literature, journalism, theater, and the educational system. The media became saturated with messages of blame and scorn for the Jews, who were described as the cause of Germany's economic and political problems. Not content with controlling the content and means of expression in Germany, the Nazi regime also actively suppressed other points of view. As early as 1933, they sent to prison and concentration camps their perceived political opponents.

Propaganda became an essential tool that enabled the gruesome reality of the Holocaust. By labeling Jews as "subhuman," the Nazi media justified their racial discrimination and oppression. Newspapers such as *The People's Observer*, *The Attack*, and *The Reich* depicted Jews as parasites that depleted the resources of Western civilization and contaminated the Aryan gene pool. Surprisingly, sending contradictory messages didn't weaken the effectiveness of Nazi propaganda. By describing Jews simultaneously as the greediest capitalists and as the leaders of Bolshevism, the Nazi media could reach an even broader audience and political spectrum. However, nationalism remained the Nazi movement's most effective means of manipulating public opinion in Germany. Blaming the Jews for Germany's defeat in WWI and for the country's subsequent economic collapse helped Hitler gain the support of the masses. Sometimes propaganda functioned as a cover that hid, rather than generated, information. The plan to exterminate the Jewish people was alluded to in code, as the Final Solution, and not reported to the general public.

The means of communication became as important as the message itself. The Nazis exploited modern technology to disseminate their propaganda to the general public. In his speech "Radio as the Eight Great Power," Goebbels declared, "It would not have been possible for us to take power or to use it in the ways we have without the radio." Each time Hitler invaded a foreign country, he launched a propaganda campaign that turned the facts topsy-turvy. For instance, the German media described the invasion of Poland as an act of self-defense against a belligerent enemy nation. The same distortion of truth took place shortly before and during the war with the Soviet Union, starting with Operation Barbarossa on June 22, 1941. Although Germany and the Soviet Union had signed a Nazi-Soviet pact (on August 23, 1939) that made them allies, once Germany launched a war, the Nazis justified their actions in the press as a defensive move made against Bolshevik Jews, who they claimed wanted to take over and destroy the world.

Propaganda remains a risk today even in countries that respect the freedom of expression. Given the way in which the mass media have become accessible to everyone, hateful and extremist groups can disseminate their message to the general public in democratic societies. Fortunately, the United States has in place a few limitations to the freedom of speech that may diminish the effectiveness of hate groups. The First Amendment of the U.S. Constitution declares the freedom of religion, of speech and of the press. During the twentieth century, however, this freedom of expression became subject to the following restrictions:

1. Speech (or writing) that presents "a clear and present danger" is not protected by the First Amendment.
2. Similarly, "fighting words," or speech meant to incite immediate violence, is also not protected.
3. Libel and slander, or making false statements about an individual or a group of people, don't qualify as "free speech."
4. Finally, the First Amendment no longer protects "obscenity."

Although the freedom of expression isn't absolute in democratic societies, delimiting it may not be enough to prevent hate groups from using propaganda to rise to power. What is said and printed is as important as what is censored. Offering quality information in the media—well-verified facts and thoughtful analyses and commentaries—about events that happen all over the world keeps the public informed, enabling us to become better judges of the information we're presented. Ignorance is not bliss. On the contrary, it offers a perfect context for manipulation by dangerous individuals and groups hungry for power.

Chapter Forty

A Cowardly Success

Bloodlands

Historian Timothy Snyder advances an interesting hypothesis about some of the motivations behind the Final Solution. Snyder believes that the accelerated timing of the plan to annihilate the European Jews arose from Himmler's and Heydrich's efforts to compensate for German setbacks during the war against the Soviet Union. When it became clear that the plan to conquer, starve and enslave the vast population of the Soviet Union was not moving as quickly as Hitler desired, Snyder argues,

> Heydrich and Himmler were able to turn the unfavorable battlefield situation to their advantage, by reformulating the Final Solution so that it could be carried out during a way that was not going according to plan. They understood that the war was becoming, as Hitler began to say in August 1941, a "war against the Jews." Himmler and Heydrich saw the elimination of the Jews as their task. (*Bloodlands*, 188)

When he attacked the Soviet Union in June 1941, Snyder elaborates, Hitler and his henchmen had in mind a dystopic plan for the East:

1. Conquering quickly the Soviet Union

2. Implementing a *Hunger Plan* that would blockade and starve entire areas of the Soviet Union, causing the deaths of over 30 million people

3. A Final Solution that would eliminate the Jews *after* the war was won

4. A *Generalplan Ost* in which native Germans would colonize the Western part of the Soviet Union and enslave its people to work for the German economy

Competing for Hitler's favor with Göring, Himmler began implementing these objectives in 1941. The Hunger Plan, however, didn't work as effectively as the Nazis had hoped. It achieved only partial success in Leningrad, parts of Belarus and the Ukraine. Overall, the conquest of the Soviet Union took longer than anticipated. According to Snyder, "As these utopias waned, political futures depended upon the extraction of what was feasible from the fantasies" (*Bloodlands*, 187). Himmler, eager to prove his resourcefulness in the face of Germany's defeats on the military front, engaged in an act of cowardice. He ordered the ruthless mass murder of all the Jews in the conquered territories in the Soviet Union and, soon afterward, in most of Nazified Europe.

Himmler traveled to the Soviet Union in June 1941 to make it clear to the Waffen SS troops and to the Order Police battalions that they needed to kill not only Jewish men—whom he described, en masse, as "Communist partisans"—but also women and children. Himmler and Heydrich worked closely together, engaging in a division of labor of genocide. Heydrich made arrangements for the Final Solution in Berlin, while Himmler managed the administrative details to carry it out. He directed the Waffen SS, the Einsatzgruppen and the Order Police under his control to mass shootings of Jewish civilians in the occupied regions of the Soviet Union. By August 1941, Snyder estimates, the Nazis had murdered over one million Jewish civilians in the Soviet Union. "The East," Himmler declared, "belongs to the SS" (*Bloodlands*, 189).

While Snyder's hypothesis that the earlier implementation of the Final Solution had a lot to do with Germany's setbacks in their conquest and destruction of the Soviet Union is persuasive, this argument doesn't take away from the fact that the Final Solution was a central goal for the Nazis regardless of success or failure in war. Since it was Hitler's top priority, the annihilation of the Jews would have happened had Nazi Germany won the war. However, the attack on the Soviet Union, as Snyder demonstrates, determined its earlier, strategic timing.

Chapter Forty-One

Planning a Soviet Holocaust

Stalin's Last Crime

Most people know about Hitler's virulent assault on the Jewish people, culminating in the atrocities of the Holocaust. Fewer know, however, that Stalin himself was planning a similar attack on the Soviet Jews from 1948 to 1953. Compared to Hitler, for many years, Stalin was an "equal opportunity" mass murderer. He masterminded the imprisonment, torture, show trials and death of his (real or imagined) political adversaries. Prominent officials and unknown functionaries, wealthier farmers (kulaks), the poor and hungry in Ukraine and other areas of the Soviet Union, Christian religious leaders, and Communist atheists are all groups that suffered under Stalin's reign of terror. Even the leaders of the secret police forces (NKVD), including Genrikh Yagoda and Nikolai Yezhov, were eventually purged. However, unlike Hitler and the Nazi regime, until the end of his life, Stalin didn't target the Jews specifically for being Jewish.

In fact, Jews featured prominently in the Communist leadership. When he planned to forge a Soviet-Nazi alliance, however, Stalin dismissed Maxim Litvinov, the Jewish Foreign Minister. He replaced him with Vyacheslav Molotov, the principal signatory of the Nazi-Soviet Pact of 1939. Later, in 1941, when Germany invaded the Soviet Union, Stalin manifested an uncharacteristic optimism and trust in the strength of his alliance with Hitler. The Soviet leader didn't react promptly to news of the German attack. For the first few days he isolated himself in shock and even forbade his generals from making preemptive strikes against the German forces gathered at the Soviet border. Having been deprived of information about the Nazi campaigns against the Jewish people all over Europe, millions of Soviet Jews were left vulnerable, on the path of the Nazi invaders. Although many of them managed to escape before the Germans penetrated their region, a large number of those living in the Western parts of the Soviet Union were trapped there by the rapid German advance.

Raul Hilberg documents that Stalin's decision not to evacuate civilians promptly from the areas invaded by Germany was motivated by two main considerations: "One was the prevention of a hasty flight of people. Their production was needed until the very last moment. . . . The second guideline was applied in cities whose fall was imminent. In these situations, priority for evacuation was usually given to skilled workers, managers, party functionaries, civil servants, students, intellectuals, and various professionals. . . . But there is little evidence of any Soviet attempts to evacuate Jews as such" (*Perpetrators, Victims, Bystanders*, 250–251). The refusal to evacuate civilians as quickly and efficiently as possible affected Jews more than any other groups, since they were in the greatest danger of extermination by the Nazis. At this point, however, Stalin's strategy was not directly aimed at the Jews.

All this changed between the years 1948 and 1953, when Stalin began mounting a specifically anti-Semitic campaign in the Soviet Union that, some claim, could have led to a second Holocaust. While nobody knows how far the Soviet leader would have gone with his plans, it's clear that Stalin began targeting the Jews for discrimination and abuse. There's also strong evidence that he was planning another massive purge. As usual, Stalin offered a pretext for his offensive strike. The death of a prominent Soviet official in 1948, Andrei Zhidanov, served as his justification, much as Sergey Kirov's assassination in 1934 offered Stalin a pretext to launch the Great Terror purges of 1937–1938. From 1946 to 1947, Zhidanov was probably second in command in the Soviet Union. He organized the Cominform, which set the official policy for Communist parties throughout Europe. In his role as Chairman, Zhdanov also set the tone for cultural production in the Soviet Union. He was infamous for his censorship of writers and artists, including the famous poet Anna Akhmatova.

Years later, between 1952 and 1953, Stalin used Zhdanov's death as a pretext to accuse several prominent doctors (six out of nine of which were Jewish) of conspiring to assassinate several Soviet leaders. He cast doubt upon Zhdanov's cause of death, suggesting a Jewish conspiracy. Aside from turning on the doctors themselves, including his personal physician, A. N. Vinogradov, Stalin also targeted Jewish intellectuals, whom, according to Alan Bullock, the Soviet press labeled "Zionist agents of American imperialism" (*Hitler and Stalin*, 951–952). Lydia Timashuk, a sycophant and political instigator, "discovered" the so-called Doctors' plot. She received the Order of Lenin for her false denunciations of innocent physicians. Stalin took over the case, ordering that Vinogradov be imprisoned and the other doctors tortured. The media called Soviet Jews the "enemies within." The anti-Semitic campaign and initial arrests were followed by more "spontaneous" pogroms in Ukraine.

The question remains why Stalin chose to target the Jews in his plans for new purges. Aside from his all-pervasive state of paranoia, which led him to suspect treachery and sabotage even from his closest friends and allies, there are several reasons for Stalin's anti-Semitic turn. Jonathan Brent and Vladimir Naumov, authors of *Stalin's Last Crime: The Plot against the Jewish Doctors*, 1948–1953 (New York: HarperCollins eBooks, 2010), argue that during the early 1950s, Stalin was planning an even greater purge than the one he had launched during the Great Terror (1937–1938). They maintain that Stalin was motivated by three principal considerations:

1. The need to reestablish the reins of power through terror and purge the Ministry of Security

2. The threat he saw in the establishment of the state of Israel and the dissemination of Jewish Zionism in the Soviet Union

3. The growing tension with the United States after the end of their alliance in WWII. Although the Soviet Union had recognized the state of Israel early on, Stalin perceived the U.S.-Israeli alliance as a threat to the Soviet Union

The Nazis killed approximately six million Jews during the Holocaust. The Soviet Union had a large Jewish population. According to the U.S. Holocaust Memorial Museum, about two million Jews lived in the Soviet territories. During the war, Hitler and Stalin became archenemies. Ironically, had Stalin lived long enough to carry out the planned anti-Semitic mass purges, he would have brought to fruition Hitler's dream.

Chapter Forty-Two

Lebensraum

The Second World War

Hitler's idea of *Lebensraum*—or creating more "living space" for the German people by expanding to other areas of Europe and the Soviet Union through ethnic cleansing, deportation, and genocide—was not original. This essentially colonialist concept had been around since the Middle Ages. However, the term itself was coined in the early 1900s by the German ethnographer Friedrich Ratzel. In his implementation of *Lebensraum*, Hitler transformed colonialism into a process of pillage and mass murder of unprecedented proportions. Claiming that the Germans didn't have enough room and natural resources to sustain their growing population, he wanted to build an Aryan empire by conquering large parts of Europe and the Soviet Union, including Poland, the Ukraine and Russia. In order to achieve this goal, Hitler intended to kill tens of millions of their inhabitants and enslave the rest, annihilating, and subjugating entire populations that he considered "subhuman."

To prove the so-called inferiority of the conquered nations, Hitler inverted, in a characteristic move, the process of cause and effect. He began a ruthless policy of terror, starving the captured population, humiliating them, assaulting them, imprisoning them in labor and concentration camps, and eventually killing most of them. This mistreatment dehumanized the victims, often reducing them to animal-like behavior in their hopeless struggle for survival. Hitler then launched a propaganda campaign that "demonstrated" that the behavior of the conquered people was abject and animalistic, inferior to that of the "civilized" German race.

Antony Beevor documents in *The Second World War* (New York, Little, Brown & Company, 2012) that, following Hitler's invasion of the Soviet

Union, "By February 1942, 60 percent of the 3.5 million Red Army prisoners had died of starvation, exposure or disease" (418). A quarter of the population of Belarus perished due to savage oppression by the Nazis. In addition, millions of Jews were rounded up in the conquered cities and villages and shot by the Einsatzgruppen, or incarcerated in ghettos, concentration, and death camps. Hitler aimed to achieve his top two, interrelated, goals simultaneously—namely, to create more living space for the Germans by clearing out vast areas of their native, "undesirable" populations.

Although they agreed on the basic principle of *Lebensraum*, several of the top Nazi officials disagreed about how to achieve it. Vying for influence, they offered the Fuhrer competing proposals. According to Beevor, Alfred Rosenberg, the minister of the Eastern territories, wanted to secure the cooperation of former Soviet nationalities, including Ukraine, in a joint struggle against the Soviet Union. Initially, many Ukrainians welcomed the German invasion and collaborated with the Nazis. The tide began to turn, however, when they realized that the Germans mistreated them as much as (if not more than) the Soviets. In Germany, the most "radical" views about how to achieve *Lebensraum* prevailed.

Herman Göring, appointed President of the Reichstag (1932–1945) as well as Minister (Reichminister) of Economics and Aviation, preferred the method of starving the native populations and bringing in Germans to replace them. Heinrich Himmler, the Reichführer or Chief of German Police and Commissioner for Strengthening the German Nationhood, opted for the most brutal method. He proposed ethnic cleansing through mass murder, either by shooting or gassing. In the end, Germany adopted all of these strategies.

Both Hitler and Himmler envisaged an idyllic German empire stretching to the Urals, built upon the mass murder of those they considered to be "subhuman races" (*Untermenschen*), including the Jews, Slavs, and Gypsies. The notion—and practice—of creating more *Lebensraum* for the German people turned Hitler's mad fantasy into a real nightmare. As Beevor elaborates, "Nazi ideas for the future constituted little more than a grotesque fantasy. . . . Himmler dreamed of *gemütlich* German colonies, with gardens and orchards built across the former killing grounds of his SS Einsatzgruppen. And to provide a holiday center the Crimea, renamed Gotenhau, would become the German Riviera" (418). The result of this so-called utopic vision of an Aryan master race dominating most of Europe and the Soviet Union was the horrific abuse and murder of tens of millions of innocent people, the devastation of entire cities, and villages and the destruction of natural resources that would take decades to replenish.

Chapter Forty-Three

The Siege of Leningrad and Genocide by Starvation

The Nazi siege of Leningrad lasted several years. It begun on September 8, 1941, and was lifted on January 27, 1944. For Lenigraders, this encirclement constituted 872 days of sheer torture, as many hovered on the brink between life and death. An estimated one million Russians died from starvation. Marshal Zhukov, sent by Stalin to save the city, followed the dictator's orders not to retreat. To the Russians' surprise, however, the Germans didn't advance much either. Hitler decided to kill the inhabitants of Leningrad in a slow and tortuous manner by cutting off their supply routes and starving a population of 2.5 million. He planned to wipe out the city's inhabitants, then raze Leningrad to the ground and hand over the area to his Finnish allies.

This genocide-by-starvation was therefore a premeditated decision—a crime against humanity. According to historian Max Hastings, Hitler consulted Professor Ernst Zigelemeyer, in charge of the Munich Institute of Nutrition, to find out how much food (and how many calories) the average person requires to live. Zigelemeyer informed the Fuhrer that the Soviet government would not be able to provide Lenigraders with more than 8.8 grams of bread daily, which wouldn't be sufficient for the majority of them to survive the siege. Based on this information, Hitler concluded, "It's not worth risking the lives of our troops. The Leningraders will die anyway. It is essential not to let a single person through our front line. The more of them that stay there, the sooner they will die, and then we will enter the city without trouble, without losing a single German soldier" (*Inferno*, Vintage Books, 2012). His demonic plan almost worked.

Within a matter of months, tens of thousands of Leningraders perished from hunger and cold. After a few weeks of the siege, the city was left without its coal and oil supplies, and therefore also without heat. The water reserves froze, resulting in countless deaths from thirst. The desperate population began hunting and eating birds and rats. Many ate cats and dogs. Some resorted to eating wallpaper paste, sawdust, grass cakes and even the dead. Corpses accumulated in the streets as the ground froze solid and people had little energy to bury the bodies. Hastings cites Elena Skryabina, who captures with eloquence in her diary the pangs of hunger the Leningraders suffered: "We are approaching the greatest horror. . . . Everyone is preoccupied with only one thought: where to get something edible so as not to starve to death. We have returned to prehistoric times. Life has been reduced to one thing—the hunt for food" (*Inferno*, 167).

The Soviets made some attempts to save women, children and workers, but millions were left behind. Once he realized that Hitler wasn't planning a full-scale attack of the city, Stalin called General Zhukov back to Moscow. The Soviet army, assisted by bands of partisans, eventually managed to open up a small corridor to the city in mid-January 1943. This enabled them to send barges of goods during the summer and sleds on ice paths during the winter in order to channel some life-saving supplies to the besieged city. Had they not built these improvised paths, Hitler would no doubt have achieved his murderous objective of starving the people of Leningrad.

Chapter Forty-Four

The Murderous Einsatzgruppen (Task Forces)

Israel Gutman's Resistance

The German attack on the Soviet Union on June 22, 1941, or *Operation Barbarossa*, converged with a killing campaign of the Jewish population of Europe. This wasn't a coincidence. Hitler and the Nazi leaders decided that a large-scale war would serve as the optimal cover for the slaughter of innocents. For the Nazis, this attack represented not only a conquest of living space for the Aryan race (*Lebensraum*), but also an epic war of civilizations. Hitler described it as "the decisive confrontation between two completely opposing world-views, with mass annihilation to prevent the recurrence of these ideologies" (Israel Gutman, *Resistance*. New York: Houghton Mifflin, *1994*, 99).

Germany invested a considerable force in this attack: a total of 121 military divisions, including three thousand airplanes. Hitler placed one division in particular in charge of the mass murder of civilians: the *Einsatzgruppen* (or "task forces"). They were the death squads the Nazis sent to occupied Poland to "cleanse" Eastern Europe of Jews. Initially followers of the army, the *Einsatzgruppen* were placed in 1941 under the authority of the SS. That's when they became much more effective at mass murder.

The killing units received orders from Reinhardt Heydrich (Chief of the Reich Main Security Office, including the Gestapo) and Bruno Streckenbach (Department Head of the Central Security Office of the Reich) to "wipe out" the Jews of the occupied territories. Israel Gutman documents in *Resistance* that, between 1941 and 1943, the *Einsatzgruppen* hunted down and murdered approximately 1,250,000 Jews with remarkable sang-froid and efficiency.

Nobody was safe. Men, women, children, and even infants; the rich and the poor; those living in large cities like Warsaw and those living in small villages, all were pursued like animals and killed by the *Einsatzgruppen*. The killers nabbed their victims—relying upon a network of local informants and collaborators—then often took them into a forest. There, they lined them up in front of trenches that were usually dug up by previous victims. They ordered them to remove their possessions (such as jewelry or watches) and clothes, then shot them in the back of the neck. For over a million people, these trenches became anonymous mass graves.

Perhaps one of the most astonishing aspects of this slaughter of innocents is the callousness of the *Einsatzgruppen*, who were usually ordinary individuals transformed by the Nazi regime into remorseless killers. Generally speaking, these men were not a group of sadists especially selected to perform this gruesome and cruel task. Most were "regular" Germans, joining the death squads from every enclave of society. Many, including some of their leading commanders, were educated individuals. Otto Ohlendorf, for instance, studied law and economics at the University of Leipzig and the University of Gottingen. He earned a doctorate of jurisprudence and became the Director of the Kiel Institute for the World Economy before assuming his role as Commanding Officer of *Einsatzgruppe* D. This highly educated man led the mass murders in Moldova, Ukraine, Crimea, and the North Caucus. At the Nuremberg trials, he justified the ruthless murder of infants and children by saying that they'd grow up to avenge the deaths of their parents. Like most Nazi leaders placed on trial for genocide, he expressed no remorse.

The murderous role of the *Einsatzgruppen* eventually became supplanted by the killing centers—death camps set up for the sole purpose of killing Jews, Communist prisoners, and other categories of people the Nazis regarded as "enemies" or "sub-human." Israel Gutman describes the subjection of Jews in Europe by the Nazis in terms of a three-fold process:

> One must view the first stage of the destruction of the Jews of Europe by the Einsatzgruppen as the transition from the system of terror, persecution, and severe oppression that preceded it to the indiscriminate all-inclusive murder from which only those who were needed for work in the concentration camps were exempted. (*Resistance*, 102)

One wonders about the mindset of the "ordinary men" employed in the *Einsatzgruppen*. Unlike most Germans that participated in the Holocaust, they couldn't distance themselves from the killings. Consequently, they couldn't render murder, like Adolf Eichmann and so many other administrative officials, an abstract bureaucratic process. They were as directly involved as possible in the annihilation of the Jews. Furthermore, unlike soldiers, they didn't fight an armed enemy. They attacked in a calculated and predatory fashion defenseless men, women, and children. The *Einsatzgruppen* are perhaps the most vivid proof that, in a totalitarian society bent on hatred and destruction, genocide can be perpetrated by "ordinary individuals" on a scale of magnitude and horror that are almost unimaginable.

Chapter Forty-Five

Poland's Plight

Gustaw Herling's A World Apart

In his preface to the first edition of Gustaw Herling's *A World Apart*, philosopher Bertrand Russell offers high praise for the book: "Of the many books that I have read relating the experiences of victims in Soviet prisons and labor camps, Mr. Gustaw Herling's *A World Apart* is the most impressive and the best written" (New York, Penguin Books, 1996). Indeed, this courageous and eloquent memoir can be compared to Yevgenia Ginzburg's *Journey into the Whirlwind* (1967) and Aleksandr Solzhenitsyn's *The Gulag Archipelago* (1958–1968). In *A World Apart*, Herling describes his imprisonment in a Soviet gulag between the years 1940 and 1941. This book goes beyond offering a personal account, however. It also depicts the dire situation in Poland, a country trapped between two brutal totalitarian regimes, Nazi Germany and the Soviet Union, each of which sought to exploit its people and pillage its land. In an unforgettable passage, the author vividly captures Poland's plight: "I think with horror and shame of a Europe divided into two parts by the line of the Bug, on one side of which millions of Soviet slaves prayed for liberation by the armies of Hitler, and on the other millions of victims of German concentration camps awaited deliverance by the Red Army as their last hope" (*A World Apart*, 175–176).

On September 1, 1939, Hitler invaded Poland after staging a pretext. German soldiers torched houses along the German-Polish border and blamed the Poles for the arson. Germany then attacked Poland with full force, launching 85 percent of its military might into the country, including 1.6 million soldiers. The Polish army fought valiantly, but was vastly outnumbered, having only 800,000 troops and a fraction of the weapons that the enemy had at its disposal. Poland received some verbal support from its main allies, Great Britain and France, but no effective military backing. The occupation of Poland was part and parcel of the Nazi plan: the ethnic cleansing of the Eastern Territory, the enslavement of the local populations, the exploitation of their labor and natural resources, and the creation of Lebensraum (living space) for the Aryan race.

As if the German attack from the West weren't bad enough, following the signing of the Molotov-Ribbentrop Pact on August 23, 1939, the Soviet Union also attacked Poland and occupied its Eastern side on September 17, 1939. Poland was thus torn apart by two totalitarian empires. As Marshall Edward Rydz-Smigly, the Commander-in-Chief of the Polish army, aptly stated, "With the Germans we run the risk of losing our liberty. With the Russians we will lose our soul."

In the end, Herling, along with many other Polish soldiers incarcerated by the Soviets, was saved by the two conquering regimes turning against one another, once Germany invaded the Soviet Union. The Sirkorski-Maiski pact granted amnesty to Polish prisoners of war and, as Herling puts it, "when the pact was signed, we suddenly became fighters for freedom and allies" (178). Despite suffering from starvation, exhaustion, lack of sufficient sleep and extreme cold, Herling was one of the few "lucky" ones.

The plight of Poland can be only loosely captured by the dire statistics of its double invasion and occupation. About 5.8 million Poles, a large percentage of whom were Polish Jews, died due to the Nazi occupation. The Soviets also took over about half of Poland, annexing its territory to the Soviet Union. Characteristically, Stalin enforced "Sovietization" through terror by setting up a Communist police state, taking over the industry and sending to gulags about 250,000 Polish prisoners of war. A large number of Polish soldiers were executed. The most infamous of these mass murders, which the Soviets later blamed on the Nazis, was the Katyn Massacre. Most Polish soldiers, however, were sent, like Herling, to gulags, from which few emerged alive. Out of the 12,000 Poles sent to Kolyma only about 600 survived. For most Polish prisoners of war, the Polish-Soviet alliance came too late. By the time the Sikorski-Mayski Agreement was signed and Poland found itself, once again, allied with the Soviet Union against Germany, most of them had perished, victims of one totalitarian regime or the other.

Chapter Forty-Six

Children of the War Years

Witnesses of War

Children were the most innocent casualties of WWII. Killed in concentration camps, orphaned by battles, languishing from starvation, destroyed by disease, traumatized by violence, tens of millions of children throughout Europe suffered and perished. Nicholas Stargardt's book, *Witnesses of War: Children's Lives Under the Nazis* (New York: Vintage Books, 2007), draws upon children's school assignments, journals, and letters to recreate for contemporary readers a historical picture of children's lives under Fascist regimes.

One of the most inspiring and heartbreaking accounts in the book is his account of life for the Jewish orphans in the Warsaw Ghetto and the heroic actions of their caretaker, Doctor Janusz Korczak. Caring and courageous, Korczak provided for the orphans even in the harshest conditions, resorting to begging for food from the wealthier members of the Jewish community. He stayed with the children to the end, comforting them as they boarded the cattle train on their short trip to the Treblinka death camp. Korczak refused the opportunity to survive in hiding without them. Stargardt describes how on the morning of August 6, 1942, after finding out about the Nazi plan to liquidate the children of the orphanage,

> Stefa Wilczynska and Janusz Korczak instinctively moved together to calm the children and get them to gather together their things as they had been shown. One of the teachers went out into the courtyard and obtained a quarter of an hour from the Jewish police to allow the children to pack up and come out in good order.... As they lined up in fifty rows of four abreast Korczak set off with the younger children in the lead so that they would not be outstripped by the older ones.... That day, all the children's homes in the ghetto were cleared by the Germans. (182)

Stargardt also depicts children's miserable lives in concentration camps and their uncanny powers of adaptation. Because of the wealth of documentation on the subject, he focuses in particular on the group from Theresienstadt, called "the Family Camp" in Auschwitz. This was the only camp where children were allowed to survive for a while and continued to live with their families. Ultimately, however, the entire group was killed en masse from July 10 to 12, 1944.

"Racial outsiders" were not the only victims of the Nazis, however. Even privileged categories of children—German children themselves—suffered during the Nazi regime. Toward the end of WWII, many German children were, like their parents, casualties of war. Stargardt describes, for instance, the bombing of Hamburg, which "marked a turning point in the war. Its scale was completely unprecedented, and it came at a time when both British and German governments thought that such attacks on German civilians might decide the fortunes of the war" (233). Child survivors recall feeling very frightened by the bombing, praying to stay alive. "The conjunction of sudden awakening out of deep sleep and the sound of the sirens was particularly potent," the author explains. "In Bochum, Karl-Heinz Bodecker repeated each night as he got into bed, 'May the Tommies leave us in peace tonight.' Among Ute Rau's first stumbling words were 'Quick, quick, coats, cellar'" (234). Perhaps the deepest source of suffering of German children was losing their fathers. According to Stargardt, 4,923,000 German soldiers died during the war, two thirds of them between 1944 and 1945 (337). Consequently, millions of German children of the war years grew up not knowing what it's like to have a father.

About 13 million abandoned and orphaned children were displaced during and shortly after WWII (351). Many were victims of forced evacuations, slave labor, "Germanization," concentration camps, and the few survivors of the liquidated Jewish ghettos. Although their numbers can be quantified, their suffering cannot. These children were the victims of a war that was largely outside of their control and, for the youngest among them, also beyond their power of comprehension.

Chapter Forty-Seven

Sophie's Choice

Holocaust Literature as Psychological Fiction

Sophie's Choice (New York: Vintage International, 1976) was a best seller in both of its incarnations: as the 1976 novel, written by William Styron, and as the 1982 film, directed by Alan J. Pakula. The movie starred Meryl Streep in her breakthrough role as Sophie. Streep's performance won her an Academy Award for Best Actress. To Styron's credit, Streep, as well as Pakula, had a great novel to work with. Written in a literary style reminiscent of Nabokov's *Lolita*, *Sophie's Choice* broaches somber themes: the Holocaust, the Nazi occupation of Poland (1949–1945), imprisonment in Auschwitz, tangled and pathological love affairs, post-traumatic stress disorder, mental illness, and, of course, the impossible choice alluded to in the title.

Sophie Zawistowska is a well-educated young woman from an upper-middle class Polish family. Her father is a professor with Nazi sympathies well known in Poland for his anti-Semitic treatises and her mother is a mild-mannered musician. When Poland is occupied by Nazi Germany, Sophie becomes involved, peripherally, with the Polish resistance. She rebels against her father's patronizing attitude towards her and becomes critical of his anti-Semitic views. Despite his Fascist political leanings, however, the Nazis shoot Sophie's father in their indiscriminate purge of Polish intellectuals. Soon Sophie loses her husband as well. All she has left is her two children, a boy and a girl. Eventually the SS arrests Sophie and sends her and her children to Auschwitz after discovering that she is hiding meat (food rations illegal for Poles and reserved for the German occupiers) under her coat.

Sophie's choice refers, first of all, to the selection process—determining imprisonment or death—performed by the Nazi doctors and SS officers, which prisoners underwent once they arrived at Auschwitz. The title is ironic because Sophie is deprived of any real power of choice. A sadistic SS officer puts a cruel spin on the usual concentration camp selections, in which prisoners had no say. He spares Sophie's life only to make her make confront a fate worse than death by forcing her to choose which one of her two children should live and which one should die. Under the threat that both of them would be sent to the gas chambers if she doesn't make up her mind on the spot, Sophie makes a decision that no parent should ever have to make: She chooses to save her son, thus dooming her daughter.

This dire choice forms the fulcrum of the movie, but, despite the book's title, it is not the focal point of the novel. The book focuses instead on the recurrent traumas that Sophie experiences, related not only to her sufferings in the concentration camp and the painful choice she was forced to make, but also to her problematic relationship with her father, which shapes the rest of her life. Time and time again, Sophie chooses the wrong kind of man. Once she arrives at Auschwitz, the young woman manages to obtain a job in the Kommandant's mansion. She even has several furtive, one-on-one, meetings with the infamous Rudolf Höss. Sophie's ambiguous relationship with Höss, and the manner in which the attractive blonde manages to gain his trust and persuade him to see her son, constitutes one of the most intriguing aspects of this psychological thriller. In real life, Höss was said to have had an affair with a Jewish inmate. This rumor turns out to have been false. Historian Robert Jay Lifton documents that Höss had an affair with a Polish prisoner named Eleonore Hodys. When she became pregnant, to avoid scandal, the Auschwitz Commandant ordered her locked up in a cell, hoping that she would die of starvation. Eleonore managed to survive the war and even testified against her former lover (*The Nazi Doctors*, 1986, Harper Collins Publishers, 201).

In the novel, however, Sophie's relationship with Höss could be better described as an emotional affair. It's little more than a brief exchange of confidences that carries enormous risks. In the end, the Auschwitz Commander never fulfills his promise to Sophie to facilitate a meeting with her son. Höss is dispatched to Berlin before he has the chance to intervene in Sophie's life. Rumors circulated at Auschwitz that Höss was temporarily replaced with Arthur Liebehenschel because of his affair with a prisoner. This too probably has little foundation in reality. It's more likely that Höss was transferred because of his role in a scandal involving the arrest of Maximilian Grabner. As Lifton indicates: "Grabner was implicated through an SS anticorruption investigation, originally aimed at profiteering, although it also charged him with murders beyond those authorized, notably of Polish prisoners. Grabner's exit was supported by Dr. Wirths, with whom he had confrontations over killings. Although implicated in Grabner's misdeeds, Höss was, in fact, promoted into the central concentration-camp administration" (*The Nazi Doctors*, 310).

Whatever the reason for Rudolf Höss's hasty transfer, in the novel Sophie never finds out if her son is dead or alive. But the drama of being drawn to the wrong kind of man repeats itself. Years later, in Brooklyn, Sophie falls in love with her neighbor, Nathan Landau, a Jewish American eccentric who claims to be a scientific genius on the brink of a great discovery. In reality, Nathan doesn't even have a job. Nonetheless, she's attracted to her lover's energy, his sexual desire, his romantic gifts and overtures and his intensity. When the narrator, Stingo, a novelist and their neighbor, becomes their friend, the three of them embark on an ambiguous friendship fraught with tension. Nathan's torrid passion for Sophie gradually turns to abuse, as he insults and even hits her in recurring fits of jealous rage. As Nathan's brother later reveals, the young man suffers from paranoid schizophrenia. Their pathological bond is doomed, much like Sophie's family life was during the Nazi occupation.

Sophie's Choice is a marvelously narrated historical novel that succeeds, above all, as psychological fiction. Which is only fitting. For how can any novel about the Holocaust—a historical trauma beyond measure—capture the devastation of that period without delving into the psyches of its individual victims?

Chapter Forty-Eight

An Incredible Tale of Survival

Alicia: My Story

Raul Hilberg estimates that over a million Jews living under German occupation survived the Holocaust and were still alive by the end of WWII (*Perpetrators, Victims, Bystanders*, 186). Each of their stories constitutes a minor miracle, a rare combination of fortitude and luck. Most of the million Jewish survivors were those living in Romania (in what they called the "Old Kingdom" regions) and Bulgaria. In both of these countries, the leaders of the government, for various political reasons, changed their minds about sending all Jews to concentration camps. A second group of victims that made it against all odds were those that were either liberated by the Allies from Auschwitz and other camps or escaped the grueling death marches, once the Germans evacuated the concentration camps. A third group of survivors were those who successfully hid, resisted or fled from the Nazis. Many had to adopt various disguises or aliases. They ran the risk of being shot or sent to concentration camps as soon as the Nazis and their collaborators discovered their real identities. These survivors, Hilberg observes, were usually young, in good physical condition, and had a particular psychological profile that set them apart from most victims: "The contrast may be glimpsed in three important traits: realism, rapid decision making, and tenacious holding to life" (*Perpetrators, Victims, Bystanders* 188). Because they tended to be not only incredibly lucky but also exceptionally resourceful and resilient, their stories sound incredible.

If any survivor story shows that truth can be stranger than fiction, it's Alicia Appleman-Jurman's *Alicia: My Story* (New York: Bantam, 1988). In a glowing review, *The Pittsburgh Press* called the book "as exciting as it is inspirational. In fact, a good bit of *Alicia: My Story* reads as if it were written by one of our better writers of fiction." In this autobiographical narrative, the author describes her survival against all odds in Nazi-occupied Poland. While Alicia lost one of her brothers during the Soviet occupation of Poland (when he disappeared without a trace after having been recruited for training by the Red Army), once Germany invaded Poland the situation for Jewish families worsened. The Gestapo systematically went from house to house hunting Jews, often aided by the Ukrainian police and the Nationalist guerillas (Banderovcy). The Nazis and their collaborators searched every nook and cranny of Jewish homes, including basements and attics. Sometimes crying babies would inadvertently betray the whereabouts of entire families living in hiding, condemning them to death. Jews were rounded up to be placed in Ghettos, shot on the spot, or sent to concentration camps.

Alicia was not yet a teenager when she was compelled to leave her home and go into hiding with her mother, after the Gestapo murdered her father and brothers. Over the course of the next few years, she adopted various disguises and provided not only for herself and her mother, but also helped others. To survive, she disguised herself as a peasant and worked as a field hand on several farms. Later, she aided a group of Soviet partisans who took refuge in a nearby forest.

Once the war ended, Alicia started working as a guide for *Brecha*, the Zionist Underground Railroad that smuggled Jews into Palestine. She made it her life mission to share her story. Talking about her painful past became a therapeutic, not only educational, experience. She recounts:

> As I continued talking I realized that if I were to survive at all and escape from the swamp of anguish and despair, I would have to reach out to people, to those who survived like myself, and perhaps sometime in the future, to all people. I would not be able to continue to hate, because I knew in my young heart that hate could eventually destroy me. But I would always remember what had happened to my family and to my people and would never be able to forgive those who committed the crimes. (*Alicia: My Story*, 272)

Chapter Forty-Nine

Revealing the Ugly Truth

The Holocaust in Romania

Radu Ioanid's *The Holocaust in Romania: The Destruction of Jews and Gypsies Under the Antonescu Regime, 1940–1944* (Chicago: Ivan R. Dee Publishers, 2000) has received high praise from Elie Wiesel. Wiesel writes in the foreword,

> I do not hesitate to say it: Radu Ioanid merits the recognition of all those who are interested in that history which has so lamely become known as the Holocaust. His work treats an unfortunately little-known subject: the tragic fate of the Jewish communities in Romania. Only a few historians, such as the great Raul Hilberg or Dora Litani, among others, have addressed it in their works. In fact, Radu Ioanid often leans upon them, but his work explores more fully the Evil that reigned in Transnistria, between the Bug and Dnister, the two great rivers in Ukraine. His work, based as it is on material from unpublished archives, thus constitutes a new contribution to this field. (vii)

This praise is well deserved, not least of all because the Holocaust is denied or minimized by many in Romania—strangely enough, not only by the fringe political elements (Nazi or neo-Nazi sympathizers), but also by some misguided nationalist Romanians.

The reasons for Holocaust denial in the country are complex; however, three key factors come into play:

1. Ion Antonescu, Romania's authoritarian pro-Fascist leader has been rehabilitated as a nationalist hero.

2. Some consider the tens of thousands of Jews of Bessarabia and Bukovina who perished in the Holocaust not Romanian, but Ukrainian

(even though they were under Romanian occupation during the Holocaust).

3. During the Fascist era, Romania had a unique and ambivalent history towards its Jewish population. On the one hand, Romania collaborated with Germany and sent to their deaths between 150,000 to 160,000 Jews (mostly those living in Bukovina and Bessarabia). On the other hand, Romania is one of the European countries with the most Jewish survivors: about 375,000 Jews living in Wallachia, Moldavia, and Southern Transylvania made it alive by the end of WWII.

Those who want to absolve Ion Antonescu and the country in general of responsibility for the massacre of the Jews have to contend with Radu Ioanid's compelling evidence to the contrary. Ioanid describes the pogrom in Iasi that occurred in June 1941 as "one of the most savage pogroms of WWII" (*The Holocaust in Romania*, 63). Iasi was a divided city. Half of its population was Jewish (about 50,000 out of 100,000 people). At the same time, the town was the center of Fascist political activity (being the Iron Guard headquarters). During the Iasi pogrom, over 10,000 Jews were beaten, shot, robbed, raped, and murdered. Hundreds of people were stuffed into boarded up "death trains" that traveled aimlessly for days on end without food or water provisions. Most of them died of suffocation, thirst, or starvation. The degradation of the Jews' humanity is almost indescribable. As Ioanid points out, "At one stop the inmates were permitted to drink from a pond where pigs wallowed; several fainted and drowned right there, others perished later from the ensuing gastrointestinal infections" (85). Antonescu not only allowed these atrocities to happen, but also, according to Ioanid, sent an order mandating that Jewish women and children be included in this "Action."

Unlike the German crimes against humanity, which were largely hidden from the native population, the violence in Iasi was perpetrated in plain sight of the Romanian people, many of whom participated, alongside the goons from the Iron Guard and government officials, in the looting, beating and murder of Jews. As Ioanid elaborates, "The mob's cruelty and greed too the form of truly shocking torture, rape, killing and robbery, all continuing earlier precedents but achieving spectacular new heights of barbarism" (62). The pogrom in Iasi, however, pales by comparison—at least in order of magnitude—to the Holocaust in Bessarabia and Bukovina, which began on June 1941 and resulted in about 160,000 deaths from forced deportations (to Transnistria), beatings, shootings, starvation and disease. Antonescu used the fact that Northern Bukovina had been briefly controlled by the Soviet Union (in June 1940) as a pretext to charge the Jewish inhabitants of both Bukovina and Bessarabia with collaboration with the Red Army and target them for mass deportation and murder.

Most of the Jews of Regat (Moldavia, Walachia and Southern Transylvania), being considered native "Romanian Jews," were spared from the Holocaust. However, Ioanid reminds us of significant exceptions: "About thirteen thousand Jews were murdered during the pogrom in Iasi, then the Moldavian capital. . . . During deportations from Dorohioi about twelve thousand Jewish inhabitants were sent to Transnistria, at least one half of which perished" (111). Furthermore, the Iron Guard killed 125 Jews in the Bucharest pogrom.

Will those who do not want to believe that the Holocaust occurred in Romania, or that Ion Antonescu's anti-Semitic policies were largely responsible for it, be persuaded by Ioanid's thorough study of the subject? Probably not. Historical evidence rarely sways prejudice or ideological bias. But that is not the book's main purpose. This historical account establishes the facts of the Romanian Holocaust, to commemorate the victims and allow those who want to know what happened access to the truth.

Chapter Fifty

A Romanian Hero

The Memoirs of Wilhelm Filderman

Wilhelm Filderman, Chair of the Union of Romanian Jews and the Federation of Jewish Communities in Romania (1923–1947), should by all rights be honored as a national hero. He's the country's most influential Jewish leader as well as the person who played a key role in saving hundreds of thousands of Romanian Jews from the Holocaust. At the beginning of 1942, the Federation of Jewish Communities in Romania was dismantled and replaced by a Nazi controlled Jewish Council. The formation of the Council was supposed to facilitate the roundup and deportation of Romanian Jews to various concentration camps in Poland. A lawyer of international repute and a former high school acquaintance of Ion Antonescu, Filderman was one of the key figures that helped dissuade Antonescu from sending the entire Jewish population living in Regat (Wallachia, Moldavia, and Southern Transylvania) to their deaths in concentration camps.

Despite his best efforts, Filderman was not able to prevent Antonescu from sending almost 160,000 Jews inhabiting the Romanian-occupied regions of Bessarabia and Bukovina to concentration and resettlement camps in Transnistria. In fact, in March 1943, Antonescu deported Filderman himself to Transnistria for three months after the Jewish leader vehemently protested additional government taxes on the Jews.

Opposing totalitarianism in all its forms, Filderman also refused to support the Communist regime established in Romania after the end of WWII. He didn't join the Democratic Jewish Committee affiliated with the Communist Party and, as a result, was arrested for a short period of time in 1945. Vilified for his anti-Communist stance, Filderman escaped to France after he heard that he would be arrested once again, this time on the spurious charge of being a British agent. He spent the rest of his life in Paris, until his death in 1963. His archives were transferred to the Holocaust Museum in Israel, the *Yad Vashem* archives, as stipulated in his will. The journal reveals the author's underlying humanist and democratic motivation: "Filderman continued to see his waging war on evil and his struggle on behalf of the Jews not only as an effort for an oppressed minority, but also as part of the larger struggle for human rights" (9).

Although deeply devoted to his family, Filderman was also consumed by his duties to the Jewish people living in Romania. He worked long days, and often nights as well, using his legal training to contest Romania's draconian anti-Jewish decrees. He was not opposed to Zionism but supported Jewish assimilation more. As Ancel states, Filderman "loved Romania and could not understand why Romania did not love him and his coreligionists. . . . Filderman believed that only a modicum of goodwill was required to see the Jews' fierce desire to identify with Romanian nationalism, to be part of the country and of Romanian society" (13). He viewed Romanian Jews, whose families had in many cases lived in the country for centuries, as Romanian citizens and fought to obtain for them the same civil rights as those enjoyed by ethnic Romanians. The emergence of Fascism—particularly after the rise to power of the Iron Guard in 1927 and of the Ion Antonescu regime in 1940—transformed Filderman's legal battles for civic equality into a heroic fight for Jewish survival.

Chapter Fifty-One

Ion Antonescu

Hitler's Forgotten Ally

Ion Antonescu remains one of the most controversial political figures in modern Romanian history. He was the country's authoritarian military ruler from September 1940 to August 1944. He was also Adolf Hitler's unwavering ally and friend during WWII. Described by some as one of the biggest mass murderers of the Holocaust and hailed by others as a national hero, it is difficult to reach a consensus regarding Ion Antonescu. Dennis Deletant's political history, *Hitler's Forgotten Ally: Ion Antonescu and His Regime, Romania 1940–1944*, sheds light upon the darkest period of Romania's past by focusing upon the views and policies of this ambiguous political figure.

Deletant claims that Antonescu was responsible for the death of "between 250,000 and 290,000 Jews and between 10,000 and 20,000 Romas" in the Romanian-occupied regions of Bukovina and Bessarabia. Correcting Deletant's figures, Radu Ioanid estimates that between 150,000 to 160,000 Jews died en route to or in Transnistria. Because the Soviet Communist army took over these regions between June 28 and July 1940, Romanians regarded their inhabitants—particularly the Jews—with suspicion. The Antonescu regime considered them to be disloyal to Romania and sympathetic to "the Bolsheviks" (whether or not they actually were Communist sympathizers, which most of them weren't). Antonescu's racial policies, closely aligned with those of the Nazi regime, caused unbelievable suffering and led to the deaths of tens of thousands of Jewish inhabitants of Bessarabia and Bukovina. Jews living in Greater Romania perished in death trains or during forced marches; were shot by the German *Einsatzgruppen* (Task Forces) and by Romanian troops, or died of starvation, cold and diseases once deported to concentration and refugee camps in Transnistria (the strip of land between the river Dniester and the Eastern Moldavian border with Ukraine).

While Romania under the Antonescu regime became infamous for launching one of the most devastating genocide of Jews in Europe, it also distinguished itself as the country with the greatest number of Jewish survivors in Nazi-dominated Europe. According to Deletant, "up to 375,000 Romanian Jews," living in what is called "Regat" or "Old Kingdom" Romania (Wallachia, Moldavia and Southern Transylvania), were saved from deportation to concentration camps in Poland by Antonescu's ethnic policies. Deletant's book explores this apparent paradox by analyzing the mercurial figure of Ion Antonescu and his shifting policies.

One thing seems pretty clear, however (and one of the main reasons why, despite his ethnic cleansing of Jews, many Romanians continue to see Ion Antonescu as a hero): the Marshal's policies consistently prioritized Romania's national interests. His decisions changed with shifting political alliances and military circumstances. Antonescu sided with Hitler once he saw that remaining allied with France and England could not guarantee Romania's national security.

Although allied with Nazi Germany, Antonescu was no Hitler. Deletant describes the Romanian Fascist regime as an authoritarian military dictatorship rather than a totalitarian state. Antonescu allowed some degree of "democratic opposition," debate and even critique of his policies (70). Quite remarkably, he corresponded and even had several meetings with Wilhelm Filderman, the President of the Federation of the Union of Jewish Communities in Romania. After his exchanges with Filderman, Antonescu agreed not to enforce many of the Nuremberg-inspired racial laws—a concession that would have been inconceivable for Hitler or any of the top Nazi leaders.

In a much-cited note to Filderman (particularly by those who want to rehabilitate Antonescu), the Marshal promises the Jewish leader that he will not harm the Jews if they, in turn, do not sabotage his regime. In September 1940, Antonescu writes, "I assure Mr. Filderman of this and I also assure him that if his co-religionists neither sabotage the regime openly nor behind the scene, nor politically, nor economically, the Jewish population will have nothing to suffer" (104).

Filderman thanks Antonescu on behalf of his co-religionists for his promises and assures him, in turn, of the loyalty of Jewish Romanians. He states, "Moved by the most sincere sentiments towards the throne and the country, the Jewish population of Romania wishes you a fruitful and peaceful rule and assures you that it will fulfill its duties faithfully and loyally" (59). Filderman's response is sometimes cited by those who want to prove that the Jewish community was grateful for Antonescu's rule. Those who want to protect Antonescu's image conveniently omit to mention, however, the mass deportations, shootings and internment in concentration camps of nearly two hundred thousand Jews from Bukovina and Bessarabia, among many other human rights violations.

Although Filderman tried to dissuade Antonescu from enacting these murderous racial policies, his efforts proved futile. "Under Antonescu," Deletant goes on to state, "Transnistria was the graveyard of an estimated figure of 220,000–260,000 Jews, and up to 20,000 Romas. Most of these deaths resulted from inhumane treatment and a callous disregard for life rather than industrialized killing. . . . The toll increased dramatically with the murder by shooting of thousands of Jews in Transnistria in December 1941 and January 1942 on the orders of the Romanian authorities there" (171). Once again, according to Radu Ioanid, the number of fatalities in Transnistria (more accurately) reached up to 160,000 deaths.

So why did the Romanian Fascist leader refuse to give in to Nazi pressure to deport *all* Romanian Jews to concentration camps in Poland, where most would have perished? Deletant mentions several factors:

1. The tide of the war changed, after the battle of Stalingrad (August 1942–February 1943), in favor of the Allies

2. Pressure from the United States on behalf of the Romanian Jews

3. The fact that Antonescu regarded the Jews from mainland Romania as more assimilated and thus more "authentically Romanian" than the Jews in the regions of Bukovina and Bessarabia

4. The warranted fear that, if it stayed on the losing side of the war, Romania would be conquered by the Soviet Union and turned into a Communist satellite

5. Filderman's repeated pleas and interventions on behalf of the Romanian Jews

6. The argument (applicable up to the spring of 1944) that the Hungarian Jews hadn't been deported and that Romanian Jews shouldn't be treated any worse than them

7. The need to make autonomous decisions based on national interests

8. The humanitarian pleas of the exiled Queen Helen of Romania on half of the Jewish community in her country

Ultimately, despite his tactical machinations, what the Marshal feared came to pass. Following a *coup d'état*, Antonescu was tried and executed on June 1, 1946, along with several top officials of his regime, by a new Soviet-led leadership. Many contemporary Romanians have more distaste for the previous Communist regime than for Antonescu's Fascist dictatorship. So what is

Deletant's historical verdict about Ion Antonescu? Judged by nationalist standards, there's no question that he attempted to defend and even increase Romania's boundaries and uphold its *perceived* interests. Judged by moral standards, however, Antonescu is both a murderer and a sparer of Jews.

The Marshal's earlier policies caused the suffering and deaths of tens of thousands of Jews and Romas in Bessarabia and Bukovina. But the virulently anti-Semitic leaders of the Iron Guard would probably have been far worse. Thus, from a consequentialist perspective, Antonescu's ethnic policies also saved the lives of hundreds of thousands of Jews from "Old Kingdom" Romania. Moreover, Antonescu's friendship with Hitler—and the Fuhrer's implicit trust in him—paradoxically contributed to sparing the lives of many Romanian Jews at a critical time (during the spring and summer of 1944) when the Hungarian Jews were sent to die in concentration camps in Poland once the Nazis invaded their country.

Chapter Fifty-Two

Anti-Semitism in Romania

The Journal of Mihai Sebastian

The journal of the Jewish essayist, playwright and novelist Mihai Sebastian is still seeped in controversy in his native country, Romania. This journal, which the author wrote from 1935 to 1944, was so taboo that it wasn't published until 1998, in French, by Editions Stock. The Ivan R. Dee English edition appeared in 2000, increasing the diary's international exposure along with the controversy surrounding it. *The Journal 1935–1944: The Fascist Years* is particularly problematic for many Romanian readers. It depicts the regimes that allied themselves with the Nazis as well as some of Romania's most notable writers and philosophers—Emil Cioran, Mircea Eliade, and Camil Petrescu—in a negative light. Sebastian's lucid picture of the Fascist influence in his native country could offend Romanian readers on several levels.

As previously mentioned, many Romanians with nationalist leanings view Ion Antonescu as a national hero that protected the country's interests in a challenging political context. Furthermore, even Romanians without particularly strong nationalist feelings take pride in Romania's leading twentieth-century intellectuals, particularly Emil Cioran, Mircea Eliade, and Camil Petrescu. Some of them do not take kindly to a frank discussion of these authors' pro-Nazi and anti-Semitic views in so far as that casts doubt on their merit as writers and on their characters. This thorny subject was also brought up with reference to Eliade and other leading intellectuals of the time in the volume *Tainted Greatness: Antisemitism and Cultural Heroes* (edited by Nancy Harrowitz, Temple University Press, 1994).

Like the contributors to this volume, I believe that national pride or intellectual merit are not good reasons to shy away from a critique of the anti-

Semitic views of these cultural figures. The fact that Mihai Sebastian was himself an important writer in the country and accepted as a friend by notable Romanian authors gives us an inside look into the cultural and political atmosphere of the times. His journal is interesting from both a historical and a philosophical perspective. It raises questions about Romania's alliance with the Nazis and simultaneously explores the relation between morality and intellectual merit in a similar manner that discussions of Heidegger's role in anti-Semitic and pro-Nazi discourses do (See Philip Oltermann's excellent article on this subject, published in *The Guardian* on March 12, 2014).

Mihai Sebastian was born Iosif Mendel Hechter in 1907 to a Jewish family in Braila, Romania. He managed to survive Fascism, WWII and the Holocaust only to die, absurdly, in a car accident in 1945. Sebastian studied law in Bucharest and mingled with the country's literary elite. His journal discusses his friendships with Emil Cioran, Mircea Eliade, Camil Petrescu, and Eugene Ionesco. Of these Romanian authors, only Eugene Ionesco was critical of Fascism. Years later, in 1959, he even published a political drama about totalitarianism, *Rhinocéros*, in which he described his friends' strange transformations under the pressure—and lure—of Fascism. Being Jewish in an epoch when Judaism was equivalent to a crime punishable by imprisonment, deportation and even death, Sebastian had ambivalent relationships with Cioran, Eliade, and Petrescu, writers who expressed anti-Semitic views and were seduced by a toxic combination of Fascist and nationalist ideologies. At one point, Sebastian expresses shock after reading an article by Mircea Eliade in support of the Romanian Fascists, titled "Why I Believe in the Victory of the Legionary Movement," published on December 17, 1937 in *Buna Vestire* (year I, no. 244). On several occasions, Sebastian expresses in his journal the hope that personal bonds of friendship can shift his friends' anti-Semitic perspectives. He tries to persuade Camil Petrescu—to no avail—that his anti-Semitism is irrational:

> Thursday, 25 [June] 1936. When we left Capsa we went a few steps down the street and he repeated what he thought of the latest anti-Semitic attacks. . . . He went on to say: "My dear man, the Jews provoke things: they have a dubious attitude and get mixed up in things that don't concern them. They are too nationalistic." "You should make up your mind, Camil. Are they nationalists or are they Communists?" "Wow, you're really something, you know? . . . What else is Communism but the imperialism of Jews?" (60) Disappointed that Petrescu wouldn't listen to reason, Sebastian notes, perplexed: That is Camil Petrescu speaking. Camil Petrescu is one of the finest minds in Romania. Camil Petrescu is one of the most sensitive creatures in Romania. (60)

Facing prejudice from one's peers is one thing; facing the prospect of imprisonment or even death is quite another. Between 1935 and 1941, the political situation deteriorates significantly for Jews in Romania (and most of Europe as well). In August 1941, Sebastian finds himself in grave danger of being sent to labor camp just for being Jewish. He's well aware of the probable link between deportation and extermination: "The alarm I felt at first is returning. Are we again facing a mass roundup of Jews? Internment camps? Extermination?" (389). Like most Jews from "Old Kingdom" Romania, however, Sebastian escapes due to a series of shifts in government policies and political alliances.

I believe that, despite its trenchant critiques, the journal of Mihai Sebastian shouldn't be judged only as an indictment of the political ideology of some of Romania's leading intellectual figures and of the country at large. Written in a lyrical and contemplative style reminiscent of Marcel Proust, a writer that Sebastian greatly admired, the journal also captures the author's great appreciation of classical music, the cultural activities of the times, as well as his intriguing and often tumultuous love affairs, which he compares to the vicissitudes of passion described in *A la recherché du temps perdu*.

As a memoir with political and ethical implications, Sebastian's journal reminds us that morality and intellectual merit don't necessarily go together. Even great intellectuals sometimes espouse chauvinist views. This book offers a deeper understanding of Romania's controversial, pro-Fascist years, from the perspective of a Jewish writer caught in the middle of cataclysmic events that he had the opportunity, lucidity and talent to describe exceptionally well.

Chapter Fifty-Three

Heroism in Hell

Resistance: The Warsaw Ghetto Uprising

It is difficult to imagine a more hellish environment than the Warsaw Jewish Ghetto created by the Nazis in the fall of 1940 and completely destroyed, along with nearly 300,000 of its 400,000 inhabitants, by the summer of 1942. The Warsaw Ghetto was extraordinary in many respects. It was the largest Jewish ghetto in the Nazi occupied territories. It was therefore also one of the largest sites of torture, predation and mass murder of Jews, 254,000 of whom were eventually sent to the Treblinka death camp. The Warsaw Ghetto was also the site of the greatest Jewish resistance against the Nazis. As Israel Gutman, author of *Resistance: The Warsaw Ghetto Uprising* states, "The Uprising represents defiance and great sacrifice in a world characterized by destruction and death" (New York, Houghton Mifflin Company, 1994, xi).

The destruction came piecemeal, creating an atmosphere of psychological torture for the Jewish population of Warsaw. On October 16, 1940, the process of ethnic cleansing began. The Nazis herded hundreds of thousands of Jews, constituting about a third of the population of Warsaw, into a tiny area that covered less than three percent of the city's living space. People were forced to leave their homes, most of their property, their neighbors, and their friends as well as abandon their jobs and businesses. Governor-General Hans Frank ordered the building of the wall in mid-November, sealing off the Warsaw Ghetto from the outside world. The SS shot on the spot anyone seen attempting to escape from the Ghetto.

Adam Czerniakow, an engineer by profession, was named the head of the Judenrat (the Jewish Council). He had to contend with lack of sufficient food and shelter, disease and starvation. He was also pressured by the Nazis to send Jewish men to forced labor under horrific conditions, and eventually was obliged to deport most of the Jews of the Ghetto, including babies and children, to death camps. On July 1942, Czerniakow couldn't take the pressure and guilt of this macabre role. He committed suicide, leaving behind a note to his wife in which he stated that he could not collaborate with the Nazis in the murder of Jewish children.

Immediately following his death, even the orphaned children he had tried so hard to protect were sent to die at Treblinka. In an incredibly moving passage, Gutman describes the dignity with which the orphans left to die, led by their beloved leader and father-figure, the Director of the orphanage, Dr. Janusz Korczak:

> They marched through the ghetto to the *Umschlagplatz* where they joined thousands of people waiting without shade, water, or shelter in the hot August sun. The children did not cry out. They walked quietly in forty-eight rows of four. One eyewitness recalled, "This was no march to the train cars but rather the mute protest against the murderous regime . . . a process the like of which no human eye had witnessed." (*Resistance*, 139–140)

For those left behind in the Warsaw Ghetto following the large wave of deportations, the moment for resistance had arrived. As long as they had a modicum of hope left, the Jews didn't revolt against their Nazi oppressors. They had the welfare of their spouses, parents, and children to think of, whom they mistakenly believed they could save by cooperating with the Germans. Most clung to the false hopes fostered by the Nazis through a campaign of misinformation. Furthermore, the conditions in the Ghetto weren't conducive to resistance. Isolated from any source of income or help, starved, overworked, and continually preyed upon by the Nazis, for two years the Jews of the Warsaw Ghetto fought for survival. Even before the mass deportations began, the conditions were so bad that about 100,000 Jews died of famine, cold, or disease. Only once the deportations to Treblinka wiped out most of the Jewish population, along with the last shred of hope, did the remaining Jews—mostly young men and women—decide it was time to take action. They fought heroically, to the death, against the much better armed Nazis.

Based on their previous experience, the Germans didn't expect to encounter Jewish resistance. On January 18, 1943, they entered the Ghetto after a four-month reprieve, to resume deportations and send most of the remaining Jews to Treblinka. This time, however, the few thousand Jews left in the Ghetto knew they had nothing left to lose. Abba Kovner, a partisan fighter and well-known poet, spurred them on with these unforgettable words:

> We will not be led like sheep to slaughter. True, we are weak and helpless, but the only response to the murderer is revolt! Brothers! It is better to die fighting

like free men than to live at the mercy of the murderers. Arise! Arise with your last breath. (*Resistance*, 102)

The Jewish fighters, organized by the ZOB (Jewish Combat Organization) and the ZZW (Jewish Military Union), fought back with all their might. They used the few guns they had at their disposal and homemade bombs to ward off the Nazis. In the first attack, a few SS soldiers were killed and several were wounded. The Nazis momentarily withdrew, only to return a few days later, on the eve of Passover (April 19, 1943), with greater forces and more ammunition, weapons, and tanks. Their order from Himmler was crystal clear: the total destruction of the Warsaw Ghetto and its inhabitants. The Nazis proceeded to hunt down the remaining Jews and burn the Ghetto to the ground.

The Jewish resistance fighters, led by Mordecai Anielewicz, Yitzhak Zuckerman and Marek Edelman, fought bravely. They built a network of tunnels underground and created safe havens even on rooftops, to be reached with ladders. They returned fire on their attackers, even though the Germans were far more numerous and better armed. As the Nazis scorched the Ghetto, the bunkers, "which had been planned and equipped to provide refuge for months, became burning cages without air, water, or food" (*Resistance*, 236). Israel Gutman's moving historical account of the Warsaw Ghetto uprising shows that the Jews did, indeed, fight their oppressors and offers an unforgettable portrayal of heroism in hell.

Chapter Fifty-Four

Privilege and Persecution

The Diary of Mary Berg

The Diary of Mary Berg, a Polish survivor (of American origins) of the Warsaw Ghetto, contains entries from October 1939 to March 1944, offering firsthand details about the Nazi occupation of Poland and the establishment and destruction of the Warsaw Ghetto, where hundreds of thousands of Polish Jews lost their lives. Published in 1945 by L. B. Fisher, the diary initially received considerable media coverage but went out of print in 1950. Thereafter, the author declined opportunities to discuss her experiences of the Holocaust and sometimes even denied the diary's existence. Nonetheless, the book resurfaced in 2006, published by *Oneworld Publications* under the title *The Diary of Mary Berg: Growing Up in the Warsaw Ghetto*, edited by S. L. Shneiderman, with an introduction by Susan Pentlin. Shneiderman had also translated the original diary from Polish into Yiddish and hired Norbert Guterman and Sylvia Glass to translate the Polish edition into English.

The diary took the spotlight again in a *New York Times* article by Jennifer Schuessler entitled "Survivor Who Hated the Spotlight" (published on November 10, 2014), which covered the recent auction of Mary Berg's private photographs due to be sold by Doyle New York, a Manhattan auction house. How did these photographs resurface? Ms. Berg passed away in 2013. A Pennsylvania antique dealer bought her photographs, which had an estimated value of thousands of dollars, at an estate sale for only ten dollars. After relatives heard the news of the planned auction, they contacted Doyle. The auction house cancelled the event, which had been scheduled for November 24, 2014. Schuessler cites Rachel B. Goldman, Assistant Professor of History at the College of New Jersey, who maintains that the auction provoked a sense of outrage. She explains why: "This could set a tragic precedent of less

Holocaust material being put in archives and instead ending up in private hands—including the wrong private hands, I might add" (Schuessler).

Berg's photographs, like the diary itself, offer an invaluable glimpse into the horrific lives of even the most privileged inhabitants of the Warsaw Ghetto. Coming from an affluent family (her father was a successful art dealer and collector of European masters such as Poussin and Delacroix), Mary Berg was especially fortunate to have a mother who was a U.S. citizen. The Nazis generally treated Americans differently from their Polish captives, in an effort to launch a propaganda campaign that hid from the American press details about the persecution and massacre of European Jews. Mary Berg's diary was one of the first eyewitness accounts of the Holocaust in Poland. It describes the tremendous duress of the hundreds of thousands of Jews trapped by the Nazis in the Warsaw Ghetto as well as the heroic Warsaw Ghetto uprising, which Mary received news about from friends.

Originally from Lodz, where the Nazis had already set up a Jewish Ghetto, Mary moved to Warsaw with her family, hoping that life would be better there. In November 1940, however, the Nazis established the Warsaw Ghetto, where Mary was held captive along with her family until a few days before the mass deportations to concentration camps began, in the summer of 1942. She witnessed the brutality, beatings, and random shootings of countless innocent civilians. She observed from her window people being forcibly deported to Treblinka and Auschwitz. She saw helpless children reduced to skin and bones by hunger and disease. She barely escaped death herself. Due to her mother's American citizenship, Mary, her parents, and her sister were sent to a camp in Vittel, France, which, as she states in her journal, seemed like "paradise" compared to the hardship and horror of life in the Ghetto.

Mary Berg's diary offers a unique testimony about privilege and persecution in the Warsaw Ghetto. Initially the wealthy and well-connected members of the community could buy jobs, exemptions from forced labor and contraband food. As members of the upper class, Mary and her friends helped organize charity talent shows, which not only gathered donations to feed some of the orphaned children and the starving poor in the Ghetto, but also raised public morale. Eventually, however, as the Nazis began implementing the Final Solution, even the privileged faced the dangers of starvation, deportation, and death.

Mary Berg was not only an astute observer of these historical events, but also a compassionate person. Even though she and her family were well off, she felt guilty about having enough to eat while so many were starving and did her best to help those in need. After her family escaped the Warsaw Ghetto, Mary continued to be haunted by nightmares about the hundreds of thousands of innocent human beings who lost their lives there.

Chapter Fifty-Five

Janusz Korczak

The King of the Children of the Warsaw Ghetto

Joseph Stalin once told U.S. Ambassador Averill Harriman "the death of one man is a tragedy, the death of millions is a statistic." Perhaps this is why readers react much more sympathetically to the personal account of the Holocaust in *The Diary of Anne Frank* than to any other history or political science book on the subject. Likewise, the deaths of Janusz Korczak and the nearly two hundred orphans he took care of are far from being abstract statistics. They constitute one of the most tragic episodes of Holocaust history, recorded both in Korczak's diary describing their lives in the Warsaw Ghetto (*Ghetto Diary*. New Haven: Yale University Press, 2003) and in a beautifully written biography by Betty Jean Lifton (*The King of Children: A Biography of Janusz Korczak*. New York: Farrar, Straus and Giroux, 1988). Janusz Korczak, born Henryk Goldszmit, was a Jewish educator, doctor and author of children's books and pedagogy. He became famous for his writing in Poland long before he perished at Treblinka. Korczak devoted his entire life to taking care of thousands of orphaned and destitute children. He worked first as a pediatrician, then as a leader of the Orphans' Society. There he met Stefania Wilczynska, the woman who would become his closest friend and collaborator.

In 1911, Korczak became the Director of an orphanage for Jewish children. In this context, he implemented some of the principles elaborated in his books: namely, that children should be encouraged rather than punished and that they need a combination of guidance and autonomy to become decent human beings. This was especially true of the thousands of homeless and hungry street urchins that Korczak and Wilczynska raised, fed, and educated over the course of their lives. Using as a role model Korczak's books, the orphans created a "Children's Republic." This was not a utopia. It was a place where the children had a lot of say in their upbringing and education, forming their own parliament, court and newspaper. A keen child psychologist, Korczak also encouraged the orphans to write a diary where they learned to express their fears and sadness without allowing these emotions to dominate their lives. He built for them a state-of-the art orphanage, which was one of the first buildings with electricity and running water in Warsaw.

Not long after the German invasion of Poland in 1939, the Nazis decreed the establishment of the Warsaw Ghetto on October 12, 1940. Korczak was obliged to move his orphanage from the Polish section of town, on 92 Krochmalna Street, to a smaller building on 33 Chlodna Street within the Ghetto walls, and later to an even tinier place on 16 Sienna Street. Even in the face of incredible hardship, disease, and starvation, Korczak struggled daily to feed, clothe, educate, and comfort the nearly 200 orphans under his care. He would solicit food and donations from the wealthier members of the Ghetto and stage plays and other cultural activities in order to foster some semblance of normalcy in disastrous conditions. Although several of his Polish former students and friends offered him false papers to escape the Warsaw Ghetto, Korczak refused to abandon the children.

Even the most cynical couldn't have predicted that the Germans would send the thousands of orphans living in the Warsaw Ghetto to their deaths at Treblinka. On August 6, 1942, the Nazis took Korczak, his staff and the children by surprise when they stormed into the orphanage and ordered them to march to the gathering place at the train station, for deportation to the East. Betty Jean Lifton vividly describes the orphans' sad procession:

> The Germans had taken a roll call: one hundred and ninety-two children and ten adults. Korczak was at the head of this little army, the tattered remnants of the generations of moral soldiers he had raised in his children's republic. He held five-year-old Romcia in one arm, and perhaps Szymonek Jakubowicz, to whom he had dedicated the story of planet Ro, by the other. Stefa followed a little way back with the nine-to twelve-year-olds…As the children followed Korczak away from the orphanage, one of the teachers started singing a marching song, and everyone joined in: "Though the storm howls around us, let us keep our heads high." (*The King of the Children*, 340)

Although Janusz Korczak could not save his beloved orphans from the gas chambers, he gave them one last gift: the comfort of facing their deaths with dignity and courage.

Chapter Fifty-Six

The Pianist

The Extraordinary Story of Survival in Warsaw

"Until *The Pianist*, I have never read a piece so moving that I had to bring it to the screen," declared the award-winning movie director Roman Polanski, himself a child survivor of the Krakow Jewish Ghetto, from which he escaped following his mother's death. The story Polanski would make into an unforgettable film in 2002 is the war journal of the Jewish pianist Wladyslaw Szpilman and his tale of survival (*The Pianist*, Wladyslaw Szpilman, New York: Picador Press, 1999). Szpilman lived through the Nazi occupation of Poland between 1939 and 1945. His family was rounded up in the Warsaw Ghetto and later liquidated along with its nearly half a million Jewish inhabitants. Time after time, Wladyslaw's intuition, luck, connections, and resilience save him from imminent death. His brother, sisters, and parents perished in the Treblinka death camp. The young man, however, miraculously manages to survive thanks to a last-minute intervention by a friend who works for the Jewish Ghetto Police. This friend helps him as he's about to board the cattle train to the concentration camp along with the rest of his family. To evade death yet again, Wladyslaw gets a work permit and becomes a slave laborer, along with the 50,000 working Jews (and their families) left in the Warsaw Ghetto.

Later the young man becomes involved in the Jewish resistance movement. Right before the Nazis stomp out the Warsaw Ghetto uprising, killing almost every last Jew and razing the Ghetto to the ground, Wladyslaw hides with two Polish friends, the married couple Andrez and Janina Bogucki. Once their pro-Nazi neighbor discovers him there he flees into an empty room, where he struggles to recover from jaundice and malnutrition. When in the midst of the Polish resistance his apartment is hit by bombs, he escapes from place to place in the stark and empty shell of what was once the beautiful city of Warsaw.

Just as he believes he has cheated death in finding a safer building that hadn't yet been destroyed, Wladyslaw is discovered by an elegant German officer. Had this man been a typical SS soldier, this encounter would have meant certain death for the Jewish Pole. But by a stroke of luck, this particular officer, Wilm Hosenfeld, reviles what the Nazis have done to Germany, the Jewish people and the rest of the world. Hosenfeld also happens to be a fan of classical music. Once he finds out that Wladyslaw is a musician, he asks him to play something on the grand piano. Szpilman selects *Chopin's Ballade in G Minor*. When he hears this beautiful music, the German officer is not only convinced of Wladyslaw's talent, but also deeply moved by it. He returns several times to give the starving young man some life-saving provisions.

Germans had almost lost the war by the time this fortuitous meeting between the German officer and the Jewish pianist takes place. In gratitude, Wladyslaw tells him his name, in case he's ever taken prisoner by the Poles or Russians and needs his help someday. That day comes soon enough. In a twist of fate—and role reversal—when captured by the Red Army, Wilm Hosenfeld mentions Szpilman's name to save his own life. By the time Wladyslaw finds out, however, it's too late. The Soviet prisoner of war camp had already been abandoned. Unfortunately, the pianist never gets the chance to save the officer who saved his life.

Chapter Fifty-Seven

Trapped in the Lodz Ghetto

The Cage

As the title indicates, in her Holocaust memoir, *The Cage* (Simon & Schuster, 1997), Ruth Minsky Sender compares the Lodz Ghetto to a cage. This is an apt metaphor. A medium sized city in Poland, Lodz had a relatively large Jewish population. Out of the city's nearly 700,000 inhabitants, about a quarter of a million were Jewish. The Germans established the Lodz Ghetto in February 1940. They forced the Jews who lived in other areas of Poland to abandon their homes and squeeze into the tiny, four-square-kilometer area of the Jewish Quarter. The cage became smaller and smaller as outside contact became increasingly difficult. German Police units patrolled the perimeter of the Lodz Ghetto to curtail contact between Jews and Poles.

The Ghetto walls confined thousands of human beings who were left with dwindling means of survival. Many of them, particularly those who had moved from other parts of town, were also homeless, at the mercy of the Ghetto's meager resources. To ensure that the Jews didn't receive outside help, the Germans passed severe laws to punish anyone who sold food or goods to its inhabitants. While the underground food smuggling and black market trade flourished in the Warsaw Ghetto for a while, in the Lodz Ghetto such exchanges became almost impossible. As contact with the Poles was strictly prohibited, the Jewish inhabitants were at the mercy of the Germans for all the resources they needed to survive.

To make matters worse, the Lodz Ghetto was governed by a Jewish Council whose Elder, Mordechai Chaim Rumkowski, ruled with an iron fist. One of the most colorful and controversial figures among the Jewish leaders, Rumkowski became so accustomed to exercising power within the Ghetto walls that he came to be known as "King Rumkowski." Raul Hilberg describes him as a vain autocrat hungry for power. He notes, however, that Rumkowski had some benevolent tendencies, particularly when it came to the Ghetto's orphans:

> A Zionist, he involved himself in community affairs and managed several orphanages with devotion. Widowed and childless, he became a dedicated autocrat in the ghetto. He was able to act alone, because the fear-stricken men who had replaced the murdered councilmen were merely his advisory board. . . . When bank notes were printed in the ghetto, they bore his likeness. Frequently he made speeches with phrases like "I do not like to waste words," "My plan is based on sound logic," "I have decided," "I forbid," and "My Jews." Rumkowski presided over his community through periods of starvation and deportations for almost five years. (*Perpetrators, Victims and Bystanders*, New York: HarperPerennial, 109)

In the effort to appease Hans Biebow, the ruling Nazi official in the area, and to keep the Ghetto inhabitants alive, Rumkowski established a manufacturing economy that served the German war effort. Even so, most of the inhabitants, particularly the poorer ones and those unable to work, barely had enough food to survive. Many subsisted on a starvation diet of about 900 calories a day. Malnutrition and disease thinned out the population even before the Nazis began deporting people to death camps.

Ruth (Riva) Minsky is only sixteen years old when the Nazis take her mother away. Her father had passed away from an illness. Riva, only a child herself, is left to take care of herself and her three younger brothers, including the youngest, Laibele, who suffers from tuberculosis. During the harsh Polish winter they shiver in the cold. Eventually Riva manages to find a job as a seamstress making German army uniforms. Despite being orphans, Riva and her brothers resist moving to the Ghetto orphanage or being adopted by other families. The manner in which their nuclear family clings together—with such tenacity that even the Director of the orphanage decides to give Riva custody of her brothers—constitutes one of the most moving aspects of this memoir.

During the winter, the living conditions become so harsh that the Jewish Council decides to dismantle all the old homes in order to collect firewood for the Ghetto inhabitants. Riva and her brothers, who live in an old house, are obliged to move into the room of an old grocery store with an underground cellar. This new place, though much smaller, serves them well for a while. Later they hide in the cellar, during the repeated raids by the Jewish Police looking for Jews to meet the Nazi quota for deportation. Riva and her brothers are particularly at risk since "Operation Reinhard," or the Final Solution, initially targets children, the ill, and the elderly. All those in the Lodz Ghetto deemed unfit for work by the Nazis are sent to the Chelmno death camp. Riva manages to avoid several selections by hiding. But she cannot escape for long.

In the summer of 1944, the Nazis begin to liquidate the Lodz Ghetto as the Soviet forces approach. They transport the remaining population, including the Elder himself, to Auschwitz. Although he had been promised safety and protection for his cooperation with the local Nazis, Rumkowski died in the concentration camp. Out of the nearly 200,000 inhabitants of the Lodz Ghetto, fewer than 1000 survived to be liberated by Soviet troops on January 19, 1945. Only twelve of them were children. Riva is one of them. She survived the harsh conditions in Auschwitz due to her youth, resilience, network of friends, and luck as well as the kindness of a prisoner doctor who took her to a local hospital. Her memoir offers a unique glimpse into the horrendous cage that was once the Lodz Ghetto.

Chapter Fifty-Eight

The Book Thief

Holocaust Literature as Best Seller

The Book Thief (New York: Albert A. Knopf, 2007), a novel by the Australian writer Markus Zusak, won numerous literary awards and became an international success. It was featured on *The New York Times* bestseller list for a record 230 weeks. Death characterized the Holocaust, and Death is the real narrator of this novel, which begins with the heroine's end: Liesel Meminger's death, many years after WWII, after she's lived a full life and had children and grandchildren of her own. As Death carries the elderly woman's soul to the other side, it also narrates her childhood diary.

During the late 1930s and early 1940s, Liesel is an adopted girl living in Germany. She has her first encounter with Death when her brother, Werner Meminger, who is also given up for adoption along with her, dies on the train to Molching. He's buried by the railway station. That day, Liesel's obsession with books and death begins. She picks up *The Grave Digger's Handbook*, a book dropped by the funeral director at her brother's funeral.

Shortly thereafter, the distraught girl joins what might be seen as a typical German family, with whom she quickly bonds. Liesel's adoptive father, Hans Hubermann, is a loyal German, who served during WWI. He is not sympathetic to the Nazis. Despite his reservations, Hans is enlisted in the German army during WWII. Artistic and sensitive—a painter and an accordion player—Hans probably characterizes the attitude of the vast majority of Germans, who weren't particularly anti-Semitic yet felt compelled to participate in the Nazi regime. His wife, Rosa, is a no-nonsense woman with a sharp tongue and a loving heart. She washes people's clothes to supplement their income but eventually, one by one, her customers let her go during these hard times.

Liesel also meets Max Vandenburg, a Jew hidden by the Hubermann family from the Nazis, whose father fought during WWI alongside Hans Hubermann. Liesel befriends him. When Hans becomes ill, she reads to him. He eventually recovers, the novel suggests, partly because of the power of friendship transmitted through the act of reading. Liesel and her family have a close call with the Gestapo, as soldiers search their house to see if they can use their basement as a shelter. Fortunately, they deem it too shallow and leave.

Liesel adapts well to her new family, sharing their hardships and struggles. The young girl becomes especially close friends with Rudy Steiner, a blond "Aryan" boy about her age, who develops a crush on her. Although Liesel refuses to kiss him, they embark on many adventures, which bond them to one another. Together, they become book thieves when the Mayor and his wife also fire Rosa. Their love of books and of the forbidden representing a protest against the Nazi regime and against injustice in general unites the two children.

Perhaps the most powerful character in this novel is Death itself, its main narrator. Death may be brought about by war and by the savage murders perpetrated by the Nazis, but it is not sympathetic to them. Rather, Zusak depicts Death as a Humanist, philosophical character that disapproves of senseless violence, hatred, and destruction. Death also touches upon the absurd at times, needing "a vacation" from its gruesome job during the war.

In my estimation, the novel's strength lies in its complex characterizations: the German characters in particular are nuanced. They struggle with the evils perpetrated by the Nazi regime and try to help victims. In the end, however, they too fall prey to Hitler's war; Rosa, Hans, and Rudy all die when the Hubermann house is bombed. Rudy doesn't even get to experience Liesel's first kiss, dying seconds before she declares her love for him. Only Liesel survives and gets the chance to have a full life. The novel's choppy, short sentences and disjointed, subjective structure weren't to my personal taste. But it is precisely these stylistic features that render *The Book Thief* popular with readers of all ages, particularly with younger readers, who can identify with the characters and appreciate its accessible style. Thanks to its literary success, *The Book Thief* was made into a movie directed by Brian Percival, released in November 2013. The movie, however, unlike the novel, received mixed reviews.

Chapter Fifty-Nine

The Forgotten Holocaust

The Rape of Nanking

Iris Chang's book *The Rape of Nanking: The Forgotten Holocaust of WWII* describes one of the most brutal mass murders in world history: the massacre of over 300,000 Chinese men, women, and children by Japanese soldiers in what she calls "an orgy of cruelty" in the (then) capital city of Nanking during the winter of 1937. The blood bath took place in the span of about six weeks, from December 12, 1937, to February 10, 1938. As Chang states, "Indeed, even by the standards of history's most destructive war, the Rape of Nanking represents one of the worst instances of mass extermination" (*The Rape of Nanking*, New York: Penguin books, 1997, 5). Chang describes in gruesome detail how Japanese soldiers gang raped women, ranging from girls only nine years old to elderly women in their eighties. The rapes occurred at all hours of the day and night, everywhere: in homes, streets, apartments, offices, and stores. Often young girls would die from these savage attacks. Not content with raping and humiliating women in a culture that prized female virtue, some of the Japanese soldiers went on to savagely torture their victims, maiming them, cutting off their breasts or vaginas, disemboweling them, ripping babies out of the bellies of pregnant women, and even impaling them with bayonets. Their cruelty knew no bounds.

Men were not immune from harm either. In fact, the Japanese first targeted soldiers and prisoners of war, luring them in groups of about 200 men to designated parts of the city with false promises of food, water, and humane treatment. Then, after leaving them without food and water for days and weakening their health and spirit, the Japanese soldiers rounded up the Chinese prisoners and murdered them. Sometimes these mass murders would turn into game-like killing sprees, in which some of the Japanese soldiers competed with one another to see who could kill the most prisoners. After luring Chinese soldiers to their deaths, thus depriving the city of its defense forces, the Japanese army turned their rage upon the civilian population of Nanking.

How can one begin to explain this level of brutality? Chang traces the historical roots of Japan's martial mentality, starting with the samurai warrior class. She also discusses the more recent, twentieth-century doctrine of racial superiority to the Chinese. She outlines some of the economic factors, including the depression of the 1930s, which, given the doubling of the population of Japan to 65 million persons, made it "increasingly difficult for Japan to feed its people" (26). The country's leaders came to view imperial expansion, particularly the conquest of China and its territories, as a solution to Japan's economic and demographic problems.

Ultimately, however, part of the explanation for this violence against civilians has to do, as was the case in Germany, with the malicious decisions of evil leaders ruling authoritarian societies. The Japanese leadership (and perhaps Prince Asaka himself) issued a clear order to the rank-and-file soldiers: "KILL ALL CAPTIVES" (40). This command was motivated by contempt for human life (or, at least, for the lives of the Chinese captives), as well as by practical concerns. Killing their victims would mean having fewer mouths to feed, fewer people to shelter and fewer worries about Chinese retaliation. Prince Yasuhiko Asaka (1887–1981), the temporary commander of the Japanese forces in Nanking, was known for his ruthlessness in war. Kesago Nakajima (1881–1945), the Lieutenant General of the Imperial Japanese Army largely responsible for the atrocities committed in Nanking, was even worse. By all accounts, Nakajima was a reputed sadist. According to Chang, David Bergamini describes him in *Japan's Imperial Conspiracy* as a "small Himmler of a man, a specialist in thought control, intimidation, and torture." Even his biographer, Kimura Kuninori, calls him "a beast" and "a violent man" (37).

The rape of Nanking, the Holocaust, the Stalinist purges and the countless atrocities of WWII don't prove that humanity, as a whole, is evil. However, these crimes against humanity across such radically different cultures do indicate that many individuals are capable of unleashing boundless violence in the right circumstances. As Chang observes, "Looking back upon millennia of history, it appears clear that no race or culture has a monopoly on wartime cruelty. The veneer of civilization seems to be exceedingly thin— one that can be easily stripped away, especially by the stresses of war" (55). *The Rape of Nanking* goes a long way in ensuring that "the forgotten Holocaust" will be remembered by future generations.

Chapter Sixty

A Cataclysmic War

Postwar: A History of Europe since 1945

Tony Judt's monumental history of the (post)WWII era *Postwar: A History of Europe since 1945* (New York: Penguin Books, 2005) examines the devastating effects of WWII throughout Europe during the twentieth century. *Publishers Weekly* hails the book as "the best history we have of Europe in the postwar period and not likely to be surpassed for many years. . . . One of its great virtues is that it covers the small countries as well as the large and powerful ones." *Postwar* describes the history of the Cold War, dwelling on the dissemination and eventual dismantlement of Communism. Above all, the book focuses on the devastation caused by WWII and its immediate aftermath.

Although Judt covers the destruction of European cities, he observes that this damage "was insignificant when set against the human losses. It is estimated that about thirty-six and a half million Europeans died between 1939 and 1945 from war-related causes . . . —a number that does not include deaths from natural causes in those years, nor any estimate of the numbers of children not conceived or born then or later because of the war" (*Postwar*, 17–18). Tens of millions of civilians and soldiers died from mass extermination, disease, malnutrition, forced marches, deportations, labor and concentration camps. We've already seen that the Holocaust alone claimed ten million victims, about 6 million of whom were Jewish.

Military losses also assumed staggering proportions. Judt documents that the Soviet Union lost 8.6 million fighters, Germany 4 million, Romania about 300,000. Countless Soviet soldiers died as prisoners of war after the Germans captured 5.5 million of them. Many of those who managed to survive the Nazi imprisonment were deported by Stalin to Siberia once they arrived home (*Postwar*, 18–19).

Women suffered from the ravages of war both as human beings and specifically as women. Many were raped and tortured as part of the atrocities of war and of the spoils of victory. Germany and Austria paid a heavy price for having succumbed to Nazi rule. As the German saying went, "Better enjoy the war—the peace will be terrible." According to Judt, "87,000 women in Vienna were reported by clinics and doctors to have been raped by Soviet soldiers in the three weeks following the Red Army's arrival in the city" (20).

With the farmland, electrical plants, infrastructure and even industry of so many European countries nearly destroyed, people continued to suffer after the war from hunger, polluted water supplies, and disease. Typhoid and diphtheria were especially widespread. Hospitals had insufficient supplies, staff, and resources to take care of the ill. For instance, Judt describes the situation in Poland: "for the 90,000 children of liberated Warsaw there was just one hospital, with fifty beds" (22).

One of the biggest Diasporas in history, WWII led to the expulsion, deportation, and migration of 30 million people between 1939–1942 (*Postwar*, 23). Germany, which started the war, lay in ruins by its end. Judt cites William Byford-Jones, a British officer in Germany, who observed the country's deplorable situation in 1945: "Flotsam and Jetsam! Women who had lost husbands and children, men who had lost their wives; men and women who had lost their homes and children; families who had lost vast farms and estates, shops, distilleries, factories, flour-mills, mansions. There were also little children who were alone, carrying some small bundle, with a pathetic label attached to them" (*Postwar*, 23).

The European Jews suffered the worst. Targeted for slave labor and extermination, approximately 6 million Jews lost their lives during the war. Even among the fortunate few who got to see the day of liberation from the Nazis, 4 out of 6 died a few weeks after. Their condition, Judt explains, "was beyond the experience of Western medicine" (*Postwar*, 24).

After describing the chaos and suffering of war, *Postwar* also depicts the rebirth of Europe. Indeed, part of the book's message is one of hope. Given the human devastation and the material destruction caused by WWII, it's a miracle that Western Europe managed to rebound and flourish during the twentieth century. Still under the grip of Communism, it would take Eastern Europe another half a century to recover from the war and the dangerous ideologies that almost led to the destruction of an entire continent and its people.

Chapter Sixty-One

The Cultural Revolution and the Great Leap Forward

Mao's Communist experiments, the "Great Leap Forward" (1958–1962) and the "Cultural Revolution" (1966–1972), created a disaster of unprecedented proportions in China. In *Mao's Great Famine: The History of China's Most Devastating Catastrophe, 1958–1962*, Frank Dikotter documents that nearly 32 million people starved to death as a result of the Great Leap Forward.

In an ill-conceived attempt to catch up quickly with the economy of the Soviet Union and the West in industrial production (particularly in the manufacture of steel), Mao Zedong launched China into a series of failed agricultural experiments. He mandated the forced collectivization of private farms. At the same time, he encouraged the peasants to plant significantly less, allowing about a third of their farms to remain uncultivated. Despite the imposition of internal passports branding Chinese citizens as "farmers" or "city dwellers," millions of peasants migrated to the cities, hoping to escape working for the Communist farm collectives and their often abusive and corrupt officials.

These disastrous measures, Dikotter elaborates, were compounded by the fact that grains were poorly stored and often diluted with water, to increase their weight and meet the government quotas. Out of a severely diminished agricultural supply, tons of grains rotted, were infested by vermin or caught on fire as a result of poor storage. To create the impression of prosperity, Mao earmarked for export most of China's meager agricultural production. The only stores that were well-stocked—the so-called Friendship Stores— were reserved for government officials and foreign visitors. Tens of millions of Chinese people suffered as a result of being deprived of adequate food, clothing and consumer goods. The situation became so dire that some desperate individuals sold their children to have fewer mouths to feed. Others went so far as to eat corpses or even kill the living to survive a few more days. Some became so unscrupulous that they disinterred the corpses of family members or neighbors and used them as fertilizer: "Inside the house were four large cauldrons in which corpses were being simmered into fertilizer, the extract to be evenly distributed over the fields" (173).

Obsessed with silencing all opposition, Mao penalized any individual who reported even glimmers of the truth about the massive famine decimating the country. Dikotter makes it clear that Mao became aware of the truth, but couldn't accept any critique, much less the massive failure of his grand designs for setting China on an industrial fast track: "Mao received numerous reports about hunger, disease and abuse from every corner of the country, whether personal letters mailed by courageous individuals, unsolicited complaints from local cadres or investigations undertaken on his behalf by security personnel or private secretaries" (69).

When the extent of destruction could no longer be hidden from view by oppression and propaganda, Mao, much like Stalin had before him, deflected responsibility for the program's failure on his underlings and cohorts. (84) He also purged from the government the officials who had been critical of the Great Leap Forward. Only once the famine had already claimed tens of millions of victims, in November 1960, did Mao finally begin to reverse the fatal course of forced collectivization. He restored some local markets and allowed the starving peasants to cultivate small private plots of land. It took two more years for the country to emerge from its economic crisis.

While Dikotter's book paints the big picture of the Chinese famine, Ji-li Jiang's memoir, Red Scarf Girl (New York, HarperCollins, 2004), gives readers a glimpse of totalitarian repression through a more personalized perspective. A good student living in a normal, loving family, Ji-li Jiang's life is turned upside down by the Cultural Revolution. Most of the values she had been previously taught—the values of education, loyalty, friendship, and respect for parents, grandparents, and teachers—are undermined by the Communist indoctrination sessions. Private ownership, academic achievement, and familial love become discarded values. They're called "Four Olds," a pejorative term indicating something outdated, anti-Communist and old-fashioned, according to Communist China's Orwellian "Newspeak."

Not surprisingly, the most mendacious and power-hungry students thrive in the new system, monitoring and bullying the rest. Jiang's father, whose Communist dossier is suspect because his father was a landlord, is sent to forced labor in the fields. Her mother falls victim to harrowing interrogation sessions, where she's asked to turn against husband. Her grandmother is humiliated by being ordered to sweep the streets. Setting children against parents and grandparents, the Communist officials pressure the young girl to denounce her entire family.

Wavering between feelings of compassion for her downtrodden family members and a sense of shame for being associated with them, at one point Ji-li Jiang decides to change her name. But she's not ready to abandon her loved ones, as the Communist official urges her to do. For her, loyalty and empathy prove stronger forces than the ideological indoctrination. Long before her family immigrates to the United States, this important choice signifies Ji-li Jiang's first step toward freedom.

Chapter Sixty-Two

The Killing Fields

Genocide in Cambodia

The Killing Fields (1984) is an award-winning movie based upon a horrific genocide. The Khmer Rouge, a Communist regime in Cambodia that ruled the country from 1975 to 1979, was responsible for the death of over 2 million people out of a total population of 8 million. The term "the killing fields," coined by the Cambodian journalist Dith Pran (whose life story informs the film), refers to the sites of mass murder in the country, particularly in the city Choeung Ek. The Khmer Rouge regime, led by Pol Pot (who acquired the reputation of being "the Hitler of Cambodia"), used Marxist theory as a pretext to eradicate the professional and intellectual classes from the country. They targeted teachers, doctors and ethnic minorities (especially those of Vietnamese or Chinese descent), sending them to "reeducation programs" that few survived. The regime's stated goal was to "wipe the slate clean" and start Communism "from ground zero" after eliminating capitalist institutions and their supporters. Given this austere policy, almost everyone was in danger. Something as trivial as wearing glasses could be interpreted as a sign of being "an intellectual" and doom a person to labor camp. Once there, prisoners were starved and forced to work in the fields in conditions that practically guaranteed death. Young soldiers, usually men and women from peasant families, forced prisoners to dig their own graves before executing them.

The movie *The Killing Fields* (1984), directed by Roland Joffé, conveys this mass suffering in personal terms. Based on Dith Pran's true account of being captured and imprisoned by the Khmer Rouge and his incredible escape, this historical drama shows the horrors perpetrated by the Communist regime as well as the heroism and endurance of its main character. Dr. Haing

S. Ngor, an actor who lived through the same trauma in Cambodia, plays the role of the journalist Dith Pran. For this role, he won the Academy Award for "Best Supporting Actor" in 1985. Sam Waterston assumes the role of the American journalist Sydney Schanberg, sent to Cambodia in 1973 to cover the civil war.

Ironically, the film begins with a scene in which Schanberg objects to the execution of two Khmer Rouge officers. A few years later, however, it's the Khmer Rouge that distinguishes itself in its violence and oppression. The Communist regime captures Schanberg and Pran, who have taken refuge at the French Embassy. Realizing that Pran, as a Vietnamese intellectual, will be sent to a concentration camp by the new regime, his American friends try to issue him a counterfeit passport. In a suspenseful and unforgettable scene, we see their hope dissipate as his picture on the passport literally melts before their eyes. The soldiers take Pran to the Killing Fields, a cesspool of mud and decaying corpses. In a stark juxtaposition, as Pran struggles to stay alive, his friend, Sydney Schanberg, now safely back in the United States, receives the Pulitzer Prize for his coverage of the Cambodian civil war. Although in his acknowledgement speech Schanberg pays homage to Pran, he remains guilt-ridden for leaving his friend behind.

Eventually, Pran manages to escape. He gains the trust of Phat, the man assigned to guard him, by pretending to be an uneducated peasant. To avoid raising suspicions, when his guard speaks in French to him, Pran pretends that he doesn't understand the language. Phat eventually trusts him with the safety of his own young son in case he's killed. This Communist soldier's character, it turns out, is quite complex. He tries to save several of his colleagues from being killed by other Khmer Rouge agents, but ends up shot himself. Pran escapes with Phat's son and several other prisoners. In one of the most horrific scenes of the movie, Pran's companion, holding the boy on his back, inadvertently activates a hidden mine. Pran is unable to save them from the explosion. A few days later, he reaches the border with Thailand, where he seeks refuge at a Red Cross camp. There he eventually reunites with his friend Sydney, who asks his forgiveness for having left him behind in Cambodia. "There's nothing to forgive Sydney," Pran reassures him, embracing him warmly.

This movie succeeds on several levels: as a historical film, a tension-filled drama, and a moving biographical tale about a man who suffered, along with millions of other victims, at the hands of a genocidal Communist regime. This real-life tragedy doesn't end with the relatively upbeat conclusion of the film, however. Three members of the "Oriental Lazy Boyz" gang killed the actor who played Pran's role, Haing S. Ngor, on February 25, 1996, in downtown Los Angeles. Thus the brave man who miraculously survived one of the worst genocides in human history ended up the victim of a random shooting on the streets of LA.

Chapter Sixty-Three

Genocide in Rwanda

Me Against My Brother

The question of whether or not humanity as a whole has learned a valuable moral lesson from the Holocaust was dramatically answered in the negative during the Rwandan genocide of 1994. Not only did history repeat itself, but so did world indifference to the misfortune of a million victims. In *Me Against My Brother* (New York: Routledge, 2000) journalist Scott Peterson describes the ethnic tensions and genocide in Rwanda. In the chapter "Genocide Denied" he also covers world reactions, including France's defense of the Hutu aggressors and the isolationist policies of the United States. He argues that these were important international factors that made the mass killings possible.

Above all, the author persuades us that, unlike many other ethnic tensions in Africa and the Middle East, the Rwandan genocide could have been prevented by effective U.N. involvement, since "In Rwanda Hutu extremists were often just young men with machetes or ill-disciplined soldiers" (292). As the title of the book suggests, neighbors, former friends, and even family members killed many of the victims in Rwanda. They used rudimentary weapons—most often machetes that had been previously employed for everyday household purposes and agriculture. Why did the United States refuse to intervene?

Peterson points out that a few months after giving the inaugural lecture at the U.S. Holocaust Museum in April 1993 and expressing his commitment to fight the evil of genocide throughout the world—famously stating "But as we are its [evil's] witness, so we must remain its adversary in the world in which we live"—President Bill Clinton, having just withdrawn the humiliated American troops from Somalia, urged the United Nations not to get involved in the ethnic conflict in Rwanda. Peterson elaborates, "Genocide must be organized to be effective, and in Rwanda that took time and left many traces. But Washington feared 'another Somalia,' and so the first instinct was denial that genocide was even occurring—that would have legally required action to stop it. The second instinct was to disengage entirely, as the US sought to slash UN troop numbers. The third move—at least from the part of American policy-makers—was to bully any other nation from acting" (*Me Against My Brother*, 290). In hindsight, Clinton would later declare that not attempting to put a stop to the Rwandan genocide was the biggest regret of his presidency.

Between April and September 1994, the Hutu majority in Rwanda ruthlessly massacred almost one million men, women and children of the Tutsi minority. Tensions between the two ethnic groups rose during the early 1990's over political control of the country. The Hutu government of Rwanda, backed by Belgium and France, had more or less ruled the country since their revolution against the Tutsi elite in 1959. However, the Tutsi minority in exile, led by the Rwandan Patriotic Front (RPF) under the leadership of Paul Kagame, was attempting to reaffirm power in Rwanda. The Hutu extremists, who called for a "Final Solution" to the "Tutsi problem," gained political momentum during the 1990s.

The Hutu Power movement galvanized the support of part of the army and numerous powerful politicians. The assassination of Juvenal Habyarimana (1937–1994), the third president of the Republic of Rwanda, on April 6, 1994, only stoked the Hutu extremists' hatred and increased their suspicion that the Tutsis were out to destroy them. They blamed the Tutsi-led Rwandan Patriotic Front for the crime, using the assassination of the president as a pretext for mass murder. Transmitting their message mostly via radio stations, they urged vendetta against the Tutsis as well as against moderate Hutus.

The result was atrocities that almost defy description. Nonetheless, Peterson attempts to give readers an idea of the sheer volume and violent nature of the deaths of hundreds of thousands of innocent civilians:

> In the next weeks, the death toll began to merge into a statistical mass. In this village one Tutsi survived from a population of 400; in that town some 2,800 were slaughtered; dozens of parish churches were turned into abattoirs. To fully appreciate the nature of Rwanda's mass killing, however, requires extracting the terrific agony particular to each death. That is now an impossible task. But an extermination rate of 45,000 each day means little, unless you explore and taste the charnel house yourself. (263)

The Hutu Power movement reinforced one simple, hateful message: in the political struggle with the Tutsis, it's us versus them. Either we kill them or they kill us. We've seen over and over again throughout history how this "us versus them" mentality can lead to the dehumanization of members of "enemy" ethnic or religious groups. This makes genocide not only possible, but also—in a grotesque inversion of right and wrong—a moral duty.

Me Against My Brother starkly illustrates the dangers of this Manichean mentality and, perhaps more so, the danger of lack of intervention by the rest of the world when atrocities of such magnitude occur. Genocide, Peterson points out, is not just a "humanitarian crisis"—as the international news described the Rwandan disaster—any more than mass rape in Bosnia was a "gynecological crisis." Genocide is a massive crime against humanity that reveals the moral breakdown of our civilizations in general: particularly when the world refuses to intervene and help the victims. As the UNAMIR commander in Kigali, General Romeo Dallaire, notes with regret about the Tutsi genocide in Rwanda: "The biggest crime of all is that we weren't able to keep it from happening" (290).

Chapter Sixty-Four

North Korea's State of Terror

Nothing to Envy

For those informed about the dire situation of the vast majority of people living in North Korea, it's tough to laugh along with *The Interview* (2014), an irreverent American comedy starring James Franco and Seth Rogen. This film, in which two journalists travel to Pyongyang and are recruited by the CIA to assassinate dictator Kim Jong Un, has perhaps one redeeming virtue: the publicity it generated brought some much-needed international attention to the plight of the North Korean people. In reality, however, the situation in North Korea is far from amusing.

Most of the country's 25 million inhabitants live the kind of lives depicted by George Orwell in *1984*. Divided into castes determined by their "patriotic" ranking; forced into jobs chosen by the government; brainwashed through indoctrination sessions after work for hours on end each day; fearing being turned in to the police by friends, colleagues, and family members for the slightest negative political remark and being sent to prison or labor camps, North Koreans live in a state of terror reminiscent of Orwell's Communist dystopia.

In *Nothing to Envy: Ordinary Lives in North Korea* (New York: Spiegel and Grau, Random House, 2009), journalist Barbara Demick offers a penetrating look into this nearly impermeable country. Even from hundreds of miles away, North Korea resembles a black hole: "If you look at satellite photographs of the Far East by night, you'll see a splotch curiously lacking in light. This area of darkness is the Democratic People's Republic of North Korea. Next to this mysterious black hole, South Korea, Japan, and now China fairly gleam with prosperity" (3). Demick follows the lives of six defectors from North Korea over the course of fifteen years, offering an overview of the country's history and a glimpse of its political repression through the optic of several personal interest stories.

Generations of North Koreans have never known freedom. In 1910, the Japanese Empire annexed Korea. During WWII, Koreans were subjected to unspeakable cruelty at the hands of their Japanese oppressors. Korean women and girls were forced into sexual slavery in the infamous Japanese "comfort houses," where they were repeatedly gang raped. Countless Koreans were incarcerated in prison camps, tortured, and murdered. When the war ended, Korea was divided into two parts; the North became Communist, falling under the influence of China and the Soviet Union, and the South was controlled by the United States. North Korea invaded South Korea on June 25, 1950, launching the superpowers into the Korean War, a "proxy" military struggle for influence over the Korean territory. When the Korean Armistice Agreement was signed in July 1953, the country reverted to boundaries very close to the original division between North and South Korea.

The 2.5-mile buffer zone between the two sides, called the *Korean Demilitarized Zone*, is, despite its name, the most militarized area in the world. Under the totalitarian leader Kim Il Sung, North Korea distanced itself politically from China and the Soviet Union by pursuing "Juche," an ideology of self-reliance. Most of the country's resources were channeled into its military. Today, North Korea observes a "Songun" or militaristic policy. The military comprises over a third of the population including nearly 10 million reserve and paramilitary personnel. The fall of the Soviet Union in the early 1990s sealed North Korea's economic fate. Deprived of Soviet aid, the country sank further into poverty, unemployment and widespread famine. As Demick documents, once Kim Il Sung's son, Kim Jong Un, took over control of the country after his father's death in 1994, North Korea's isolation became absolute as its political repression intensified.

Nowadays, starvation is a commonplace phenomenon. The North Koreans even have a name for the tens of thousands of starving children who resort to begging in the street to survive: they call them "little swallows." While the vast majority of the population of North Korea lives in squalor, their leader enjoys immense wealth. In an article in *The New York Times* titled "Pyongyang's Hunger Games," Joshua Stanton and Sung-Yoon Lee state that Kim Jung-Un is said to have squandered 645,800,000 dollars in 2012 on luxury goods, "including cosmetics, handbags, leather products, watches, electronics, cars and top-shelf alcohol. In that same year Mr. Kim also spent 1.3 billion dollars on his ballistic missile program" (March 7, 2014).

Demick's account personalizes the politics of North Korea by showing how it affects ordinary citizens. She narrates the life story of Mi-Ran, a young teacher. Mi-Ran fell in love like anyone living in a free country. But her options in North Korea were severely limited because, as Demick explains, "the country doesn't have a dating culture. Many marriages are still arranged, either by families or by party secretaries or bosses" (80). Mi-Ran may have felt the same emotions for the young man she cared about as do people living in free societies, but she couldn't be with him because her political dossier was tainted by the fact that her father was a South Korean POW. The young woman may have experienced empathy like most human beings do in normal circumstances, but her situation was far from normal. In a country ravaged by hunger, she watched as her students wasted away from starvation. Many disappeared without a trace from her classroom.

Barely having enough food for herself, Mi-Ran couldn't help them. Her empathy eventually gave way to indifference, a common survival tactic: "What she didn't realize is that her indifference was an acquired survival skill. In order to get through the 1990s alive, one had to suppress any impulse to share food. To avoid going insane, one had to learn to stop caring" (130). Mi-Ran regained her humanity and put the political situation of her country in proper perspective only once she immigrated to South Korea.

Even Mrs. Song, a model patriotic citizen, eventually overcame the fear and brainwashing instilled by her government. Each of the defectors interviewed by Demick eventually saw North Korea for what it is: a totalitarian country ruled by a voracious despot, whose absurd personality cult may become an object of lighthearted satire for those living in freedom, but who transforms the lives of the people of North Korea into a living nightmare.

Chapter Sixty-Five

Yad Vashem

"A Place and a Name" of Remembrance

It's impossible to write a book about "Holocaust memories" without mentioning Yad Vashem, the Holocaust memorial museum in Israel, which is dedicated to preserving the collective memories of the Holocaust and to educating the public about this historical catastrophe. The goal of the Holocaust was not only to exterminate the Jewish people. It was also to erase their memory: to efface every trace that they had perished at the hands of the Nazis and even that they had ever existed. This is why the Nazis avoided, as much as possible, leaving a written trace of their lethal commands and destroyed the evidence of their crimes. The mass murder of millions of Jews was kept, for the most part, a secret in Germany. Orders for extermination were referred to in code. Mass murder was called "the Final Solution," the process of hunting down victims to send them to concentration camps was called "Actions" or "Operations," and the extermination of the Jews was euphemistically called "Special Treatment." These orders were generally expressed verbally, from Hitler to Himmler and so on, down the chain of command. Given the Nazi emphasis upon the systematic erasure of this criminal past, it's all the more important for the Jewish people—and for the world at large—to have places of remembrance of the Holocaust.

Yad Vashem, which literally means "a place and a name," commemorates the memory of those who have perished in the Holocaust. The museum also honors those who have helped Jews escape from the Nazis. Plans for Yad Vashem began as early as 1942, with the first confirmed reports of the mass murder of Jews. In 1953, the Israeli parliament, the Knesset, unanimously passed a law establishing Yad Vashem. In 1957, the museum opened to the public. Since its inception, Yad Vashem has been one of the most visited places in Israel, along with the Western Wall (the Wailing Wall). Located on the Mount of Remembrance in Jerusalem, the museum contains a Holocaust History Museum, a Children's Memorial, a Hall of Remembrance, a Museum of Holocaust Art, an International School of Holocaust Studies, a library, a research center, and a publishing house. The section about the Holocaust contains documents, photos, and videos in English, Hebrew, German, Russian, and Arabic. The museum has several interrelated objectives:

1. Commemorating Holocaust victims, survivors, and those who have helped victims escape from the Nazis
2. Offering the most up-to-date documentation about the Holocaust
3. Conducting further research on the Holocaust
4. Educating the general public about the Holocaust

To preserve the memory of the Holocaust—or of any historical disaster—well beyond the lifespan of its victims and their families, one needs to keep those memories alive for present and future generations. Yad Vashem maintains a delicate balance between retrieving the past as accurately as possible and using modern tools of mass media communication to render that past relevant to as many people as possible.

The Nazis claimed the lives of their victims and deprived them of dignity both in life and in death. They killed them mercilessly and disposed of their bodies anonymously, tossing them into a heap, burying them in mass graves, or incinerating them. To preserve the memories of the millions of victims of Nazi extermination, one of the museum's main research tasks is to identify and honor each victim as an individual. In 2005, Yad Vashem created a permanent exhibition devoted to this purpose in the new Holocaust History Museum. The explicit goal of this vast and growing display of photographs is "identifying the men, women and children who appear in the photographic display restores names and identities to unknown faces, thereby rescuing them from anonymity" ("Anonymous No Longer: Names of Men, Women and Children Identifed in the Photographic Display in the Holocaust History Moseuem at Yad Vashem"). The Hall of Names, in particular, includes hundreds of photographs of victims of the Holocaust.

The new museum, a triangular structure with a luminous, 200-meter-long prism skylight, was designed by Moshe Safdie, a Canadian architect born in Haifa. Safdie also created the spectacular Kauffmann Center for the Performing Arts in Kansas City, The Musée de la Civilisation in Quebec City and the National Gallery of Canada in Ottawa. One of the main reasons to remember the past is to shape the future, so that younger generations learn how to identify the warning signs of the hatred and racism that engulfed previous generations. Consequently, in the words of Moshe Katzav, a former President of Israel, Yad Vashem stands as "an important signpost to all of humankind, a signpost that warns how short the distance is between hatred and murder, between racism and genocide."

Chapter Sixty-Six

An Impossible Conflict in Gaza

Rock the Casbah

The Holocaust underscored for the Jewish people the necessity of building their own nation. Deprived of full citizenship rights in many European countries and entirely stripped of human rights once the Nazis came to power, the Jews became ostracized and persecuted throughout Europe. They were branded as outsiders and eventually stomped out like "vermin" by the Nazis, even in countries they had inhabited for centuries. One of the ironies of history is that to claim a land and establish a country of their own in 1948—the state of Israel—the Jewish people had to displace another people, the Palestinians, leading to one of the most difficult conflicts in modern political history.

Nowhere was this conflict more heated than on the West Bank and in Gaza, a thin strip of land bordering Egypt and Israel. When Israel won the Six Day War against Egypt in 1967, the Israelis took control of Gaza, an area already populated by over one million Palestinian Sunni Muslims. After signing the Oslo Accords in 1993, the Palestinian Authority governed Gaza. However, Israel maintained control of its airspace, borders (with the exception of the border with Egypt) and waters, monitoring what went in and out of the area. Thus, for all practical purposes, Israel acquired enormous control over its economy. Much of the local Arab population viewed the Israeli presence as an occupation by an enemy nation. Encouraged by Hamas and other militant organizations, Palestinian youth launched their own form of protest, or "Intifada" (uprising). They threw rocks and, sometimes, Molotov cocktails into the crowds. They also engaged in suicide bombing expeditions against the Israeli forces and, sometimes, also against civilians. The Israelis, in turn, launched counterattacks and enacted punitive measures. This conflict has led to the death of civilians on both sides.

Does my brief summary sound biased? Although I attempted to be impartial, many would say that I wasn't. It's nearly impossible to describe the Israeli-Palestinian conflict objectively, without seeming to favor one side or the other. Impartiality itself tends to be viewed as a bias, since members of both communities feel that the other side behaves in an immoral and self-serving manner. Given how difficult it is to be fair to both sides, it's all the more remarkable that the independent film directed by Yariv Horowitz, *Rock the Casbah* (2013), does justice to this divisive subject.

The movie manages to capture the complexity of the conflict in Gaza during the First Intifada in 1989. Although the film is narrated from the perspective of four young Israeli soldiers sent to Gaza to suppress the uprising, it doesn't dehumanize the Palestinians. It also doesn't convey the Israeli soldiers as righteous heroes. In fact, the movie's strength—acknowledged by several film critics, including Jordan Hoffman in *film.com* and Alissa Simon in *Variety*—lies in its realism and compelling characterizations.

In Israel, most citizens over the age of eighteen are required to serve in the military. Men generally serve three years, women two. Many go willingly and gladly, others do not. In his depiction of the Israeli soldiers, Horowitz captures an entire spectrum of attitudes towards the Israeli-Arab conflict—from the ideologically patriotic stance of the Israeli commander (played by Angel Bonnani) to the ambivalent reaction of the main character Tomer (Yon Tumarkin), who for the most part is traumatized by violence, to the hot-headed hatred of Aki (Roy Nik), to the easy-going attitude of their likable leader, Ariel (Yotam Ishay), who tries to calm down his fellow soldiers when they seek vengeance against the Arabs. In fact, Ariel can't wait to complete the few weeks he has left of military service and go to Amsterdam.

The plot centers on an initial act of violence, which sparks a bigger conflict. A young Israeli soldier is crushed to death by a Palestinian youth who throws a washing machine on him from a rooftop. During the rest of the movie, four of his fellow soldiers are stationed on that roof, to prevent further violence and hunt down the man who killed their friend. This isn't an easy feat, since the perpetrator's family and friends try to hide and protect him. In the process of seeking the killer, the Israelis round up, in a more or less haphazard fashion, all the young Arab males in the area whom they suspect of being involved in acts of aggression against the state of Israel. They blindfold them, shove them into a van and take them to a Secret Service prison for interrogation.

The movie also captures the understandable resentment of the Palestinian family (a mother, father and their children) on whose roof the Israeli soldiers are stationed. Although this family is not directly involved in acts of violence, they refuse to turn in their nephew, the young man who killed the

Israeli soldier. Their little boy, not understanding what's happening, wants to play "soldier" games with the Israelis. Ostracized by their community as "collaborators" and suspected by the Israeli soldiers of protecting the enemy, this Palestinian family is caught in a Catch-22 situation that reduces the parents to despair.

Rock the Casbah maintains suspense not only through its strong characterizations, but also through the sparing use of violence. The movie includes only two main acts of physical violence: the scene of the killing of the Israeli soldier at the beginning and one at the end, both of which leave a strong impression. Above all, *Rock the Casbah* neither idealizes nor demonizes either side of this impossible conflict in the Gaza Strip.

Chapter Sixty-Seven

Anti-Semitism Today and the Assault on Democratic Values

In an article published in *The Guardian* on August 7, 2014, Jon Henley begins with an ominous headline: "Anti-Semitism is on the rise throughout Europe 'in worst times since the Nazis.'" He cites several sources for this alarming conclusion, including *Crif*, France's collective Jewish organizations, which reported that in the previous month seven synagogues were attacked, a kosher supermarket looted and crowds gathered to chant with banners "Death to Jews" and "Slit Jews' throats." In Germany, Henley pursues, people threw Molotov cocktails into the Bergische synagogue in Wuppertal, the same building where a mob led by the SS attacked the Jewish community decades earlier. These incidents are reminiscent of Kristallnacht ("Crystal Night"), when angry crowds, led by SA paramilitary forces, attacked Jews in Germany and Austria on November 9 and 10, 1938, destroying and looting Jewish-owned stores, buildings and synagogues. This anti-Semitic rampage ushered Hitler's more systematic economic and racial persecution of the Jews, paving the way for the Final Solution.

Such violent incidents led Dieter Graumann, the President of Germany's *Central Council of Jews*, to declare that "these are the worst times since the Nazi era." In France, Roger Cukierman, the President of France's *Crif*, similarly expressed concern that the severe anti-Semitic backlash goes far beyond opposition to Israel's current policies in Gaza or even to the state of Israel: "They are not screaming 'Death to the Israelis' on the streets of Paris. They are screaming 'Death to the Jews.'" As Henley explains, it's not only the Jewish communities in Europe that have serious reasons for concern. These hateful anti-Semitic outcries signal a danger for human rights and democratic institutions in general. Angela Merkel, Germany's Chancellor, rightly called the current wave of anti-Semitism "an attack on freedom and tolerance and our democratic state."

As much as such hate-filled actions and demonstrations against European Jews are cause for concern, the current situation can't be compared to Europe during the reign of Fascism. For one thing, it's reassuring that European heads of government don't endorse these hate messages and assaults. Second, I'd be interested in finding out more about who is manifesting anti-Semitic violence. If it's mostly Islamic extremists, sadly, that's to be expected.

We face a greater danger, in my estimation, when such attitudes gain ground with the mainstream public: that is to say, when the general population of European countries becomes used to the anti-Semitic rhetoric and actions and remains indifferent to them or, worse still, begins to support them. This can easily happen when legitimate humanitarian concerns—for the welfare of the Palestinian population in Gaza, for instance—turn into hatred of the Jews. I have described briefly the nature of the conflict between Israelis and Palestinians in Gaza in the previous chapter on Yariv Horowitz's film on the subject, *Rock the Casbah*.

I allude to this movie here again because an outburst of anti-Semitism in Europe in July 2014 was fanned by Israeli air strikes in Gaza that killed over 200 Palestinians (according to Palestinian sources). These strikes were launched in retaliation for over one thousand rockets fired against Israel from Gaza (according to Israeli reports). Most of us have opinions, and many of us have strong feelings, about the ongoing conflicts in the Middle East. It's perfectly defensible to disagree about this complex subject or to disapprove of the human rights violations that occur on both sides. For as long as our standards of value remain humanitarian—to defend the human rights of all people—we will be safe, as civilizations, from the ravages of another Holocaust.

The greatest danger, I believe, occurs when the mainstream public loses sight of democratic and humanitarian values and asks for the annihilation of one people (in this case, the Jews) in the name of defending the human rights of another (in this case, the Palestinians). This violation of the humanitarian standards they claim to support jeopardizes not only the Jewish population once again, but also the democratic values that underpin Western societies. It happened to the Weimar Republic and other governments after WWI and it could happen again. Those who protest Israel's policies in Gaza on humanitarian grounds while engaging in anti-Semitic actions or hate speech are showing that they don't really care about these values or causes universally. They defend the rights of one group and are prepared to trample upon the rights of another. In my opinion, defending human rights is far more important than being either pro-Israel or pro-Palestine. If we don't wish to witness another genocide, first and foremost, let us be pro-human.

Chapter Sixty-Eight

Would You Forgive the Nazi Perpetrator?

The Sunflower

Simon Wiesenthal's *The Sunflower: On the Possibilities and Limits of Forgiveness* is a parable about moral responsibility for crimes against humanity that raises the possibility of forgiving the perpetrators. The narrator describes his daily existence in the Lemberg concentration camp. The story reflects, in some respects, Wiesenthal's own experiences in several Nazi concentration camps: including Janowska, Plaszow, and Mauthausen. Although the narrative shies away from offering graphic descriptions of violence, it alludes to the sadistic mistreatment of inmates by SS officers as well as to the starvation, disease, and constant threat of being shot or selected for the crematoria that were part and parcel of the daily horrors experienced by Jewish inmates. The book, originally published by Schocken Books in 1976, has been taught for decades in schools as an introduction to the Holocaust. Written in an elegant prose, *The Sunflower* has been especially popular because it raises important questions about moral responsibility for crimes against humanity and explores the victims' capacity for forgiveness. The latter point was particularly relevant to Wiesenthal, who spent decades tracking down Nazi fugitives and bringing them to justice.

In a moment of rare beauty in his somber existence in the concentration camp, the narrator, a Jewish prisoner on his way to forced labor, sees a row of sunflowers planted on Christian soldiers' graves. In a poetic scene, the narrator describes how he's initially enthralled by the flowers' beauty, only to be later struck by its implications:

> I stared spellbound. The flower heads seemed to absorb the sun's rays like mirrors and draw them down into the darkness of the ground as my gaze wandered from the sunflower to the grave. . . . It was gaily colored and butterflies fluttered from flower to flower. . . . Were they whispering something to each flower to pass on to the soldier below? Yes, this was just what they were doing; the dead were receiving light and messages. (*The Sunflower*, Simon Wiesenthal, New York: Schocken Books, 1998, 14)

As he overcomes his sense of awe, the narrator realizes that, as a Jewish prisoner, he'll be deprived of dignity not only in life, but also in death. He'll be probably shot and tossed into a mass grave or gassed and incinerated. For him, as for millions of other Jewish prisoners, "No sunflower would ever bring light into my darkness, and no butterflies would dance above my dreadful tomb" (*The Sunflower*, 15).

When the narrator arrives at work, where he's charged with disposing of medical waste, a nurse signals him to follow her to a hospital bed. There he encounters a man enveloped in bandages, pale and thin. As this man addresses him with great difficulty, the narrator realizes that the dying patient is a young SS officer. Surprisingly, the officer begs for his forgiveness for what he's done to other Jews. Without making excuses for his behavior, he describes some of its causes. He tells him about the Nazi indoctrination sessions he attended when he was a member of Hitler Youth. He speaks of the manuscripts and speeches that depicted Jews as a "subhuman race" and called for their annihilation.

Now that he's about to die, however, the officer feels a sense of responsibility and guilt for his murderous acts against defenseless civilians. He confesses that he was part of an SS brigade that hunted Jews and forced dozens of them into a house. He then tossed hand grenades into the windows to kill them. Some people jumped, ablaze, through broken windows. Still haunted by this gruesome memory, the SS officer can't die in peace without receiving atonement from a Jew. The narrator is paralyzed by indecision. He doesn't know how to respond to the German's request.

When he returns to the camp that evening, he tells his Jewish friends about this strange encounter. Adam, an architect, finds the request preposterous given that the Nazis were murdering millions of Jews. One less Nazi, he responds. Josek, a deeply religious Jew, maintains that he'd have refused to pardon the SS officer with a clear conscience. How could his friend have forgiven atrocities of such magnitude? And who was he to speak for millions of other victims? His friends express skepticism: Why would the "Aryan Superman" need the forgiveness of a "Subhuman" Jew? they wonder. The narrator, however, sees the dying Nazi as a fellow human being. "The SS man's attitude toward me was not that of an arrogant superman. Probably I hadn't successfully conveyed all my feelings: a subhuman condemned to death at the bedside of an SS man condemned to death" (*The Sunflower*, 67).

Of course, in life, their circumstances were diametrically opposed. Still unsure of his own ethical stance, the narrator asks each of us, readers, to ask ourselves: if faced with the Nazi soldier's last request for forgiveness, "What would I have done" (*The Sunflower*, 98).

If we read the transcripts of the Nazi leaders tried for war crimes, we see that the question of guilt and forgiveness doesn't come up often for the main perpetrators. Adolf Eichmann and Rudolf Hoss, for instance, expressed no regret or compunction. They denied personal responsibility and blamed the Nazi system and their superiors for their murderous deeds. Yet for the surviving victims, the question is extremely relevant because it asks them to consider at least some of the (lower-level) perpetrators as individuals capable of genuine remorse for their crimes.

Wiesenthal's parable shows the Nazis as a diverse group that nevertheless behaved in a similar manner. Not every SS soldier hated Jews. Not every SS soldier was a ruthless sadist. Not every SS soldier gladly followed orders to butcher innocent people. Yet almost every SS soldier chose, like the officer depicted in *The Sunflower*, to follow such orders and to commit such crimes. Almost every SS soldier killed countless innocent Jews. Understanding the forces at play that made genocide possible does not mean exonerating the perpetrators of blame. But without a sociological, and historical, understanding of how tens of thousands of "ordinary" German citizens were capable of such atrocities, we are likely to overlook the vulnerabilities of our own societies.

Chapter Sixty-Nine

Could the Holocaust Happen Again?

Nazi Hunter

Alan Levy's study of the life and works of Nazi hunter and world-renowned author Simon Wiesenthal, *Nazi Hunter: The Wiesenthal File* (New York, Barnes and Noble Books, 1993), probes the question that is at the bottom of any understanding of the Holocaust: Could the Holocaust happen again? Wiesenthal's answer, expressed in several of his works, is unequivocally *yes*. It could happen again, even though it's not likely to start in the same country, or under the same conditions, or even with the same group of victims. In raising this question, Wiesenthal's underlying concern is not only will there be another Holocaust against the Jews in particular, but also against any social groups that other groups wish to obliterate. The core of Nazism was racial hatred and intolerance. The Jews were the initial and most relentlessly pursued victims, along with the Gypsies. Both groups were deemed to be "subhuman" and a plague to humanity by Nazi ideology. The Slavs, whom the Nazis also considered subhuman, were their next targets for enslavement and possible extermination. We will never know if or when the mass murder would have ended had the Nazis not been stopped in their tracks by losing the war.

Wiesenthal argues, however, that it's not accidental that the Holocaust happened primarily to the Jews, a minority group that lacked a nation and was discriminated against in most European countries. He also maintains that genocide could happen again, to the Jews or other groups of victims, if the following six conditions are met:

1. *Hatred*. According to Wiesenthal, "Hatred is the juice on which those two monsters of human history, Hitler and Stalin, survived" (23). He

argues that most of the Nazi leaders, including Eichmann, wouldn't have used their organizational skills for genocide had it not been for Hitler's rise to power.

2. *Dictatorship.* Genocide is the result of hateful sociopathic leaders who assume total or near-total power in a country. Without establishing totalitarian control of their nations, neither Hitler nor Stalin would have succeeded in killing millions of people.

3. *Bureaucracy.* Eichmann was first and foremost an efficient bureaucrat—a behind-the-desk mass murderer. The Nazi bureaucratic machine, set up in most countries controlled by or allied to Germany, enabled the extermination machinery to run smoothly.

4. *Modern technology.* Wiesenthal believes that only modern technology facilitates genocide on such a massive scale. He speculates that had this technology been available during the Spanish Inquisition, the Spaniards too might have killed the Jews en masse rather than given them the "choice" to convert or die.

5. *A world crisis or war.* Without the World War triggered by Germany's invasion of the Soviet Union, Hitler couldn't have engaged in such a massive and brazen genocide. WWII focused the Allies' energies and attention on their primary objective—winning the war—rather than on the enormous humanitarian crises caused by Fascist regimes.

6. *Minorities as victims.* Wiesenthal suggests that the targeted minority groups could be of any kind: racial, ethnic, religious or political. If a given minority group is used as a scapegoat and blamed by sociopathic rulers for their country's problems, they could become the victims of discrimination and even eventual extermination under the right circumstances. The author elaborates: "When the Turks killed a million and a half Armenians almost a hundred years ago, those six components of genocide were there and they were there, too, when the Spanish Inquisition put twenty people on a stake and burned them. And I can promise you that Hitler has studied very carefully those holocausts" (*Nazi Hunter*, 24).

The technology and mass media available to Hitler—which, of course, weren't available during the Spanish Inquisition—increased Hitler's powers of mass destruction. As Wiesenthal asks, "What will happen to this world when the haters today, the terrorists, come into possession of the technology of our time?" (*Nazi Hunter*, 25) We are still in the midst of grappling with this question, which is even more relevant today than it was when Wiesenthal first raised it.

Chapter Seventy

Ethics above Politics

It is difficult to believe that, decades later, the Holocaust remains a controversial topic. It still polarizes people and leads to heated political debates rather than generating universal moral agreement. Ironically, I think this subject becomes politicized when an essentially ethical question comes up: Who bears responsibility for it? This question tends to turn political when important historical figures—the leaders of various regimes associated with or supportive of Nazism—become, for some, nationalist symbols. The focus of discussion then changes from a defense of the millions of innocent victims to a defensive nationalist posture. However complex the political and historical considerations may have been for each country during WWII, it's important to keep in mind that the central issue at stake in the Holocaust is *universal* rather than national. The Holocaust represents the worst violation of human dignity and rights.

This is a central message of *The Diary of Anne Frank* and one of the main reasons why this journal remains so popular, generations later, throughout the world. This young girl shows us what happens to ordinary human beings when they are subject to extraordinary brutality. She also reminds us that our common humanity is, fundamentally, far more important than our political, ethnic, racial and religious differences. In one of her most poignant diary entries, Anne describes the savage hunt of Jews by the Nazis in Holland, comparing it to the slave hunts:

> Countless friends and acquaintances have gone to a terrible fate. Evening after evening the green and gray army lorries trundle past. The Germans ring at every front door to inquire if there are any Jews living in the house. If there are, then the whole family has to go at once. . . . It seems like the slave hunts of olden times. . . . In the evenings when it's dark, I often see rows of good, innocent people accompanied by crying children, walking on and on, in charge

of a couple of these chaps, bullied and knocked about until they almost drop. No one is spared—old people, babies, expectant mothers, the sick—each and all join in the march of death. (*The Diary of Anne Frank*, New York: Bantam Books, 1967, pp. 53–54)

It is remarkable, though perhaps not surprising, that the notion that injustice is injustice no matter what social group suffers from it is expressed by a thirteen-year-old child. In fact, adults were initially blind to Anne Frank's message, which almost didn't see the light of day: not even after her family friend, Miep Gies, placed it in a drawer to save it from being confiscated by the Nazis; not even once it reached the hands of her father, Otto Frank, who himself barely made it alive from Auschwitz.

Otto struggled for years to find a publisher that would print his daughter's diary. As Francine Prose recounts in *Anne Frank: The Book, the Life, the Afterlife*, "The manuscript was rejected by every editor who read it [in Holland], none of whom could imagine that readers would buy the intimate diary of a teenage girl, dead in the war" (New York: Harper Collins 2009, 77).

Eventually the diary got published in Holland, largely thanks to the praise offered by the journalist Jan Romein. In 1946, Romein wrote a moving review entitled "A Child's Voice," in which he stated that he was impressed by Anne's keen insights into human nature (*Anne Frank: The Book, the Life, the Afterlife*, 77). Even so, the diary's fate—and its extraordinary success—was far from certain in the United States. In America, as in Holland, publishers initially viewed it with skepticism. As Francine Prose continues to explain, almost every mainstream publishing house rejected Anne's diary. Editors saw it "as being too narrowly focused, too domestic, too Jewish, too boring, and above all, too likely to remind readers of what they wish to forget" (*Anne Frank: The Book, the Life, the Afterlife*, 80–81). People wanted to put the war, and its horrors, behind them.

Fortunately, two young editors identified with Anne's words and saved the book from oblivion: Judith Jones, an assistant of the Director of Doubleday (who became a famous editor at Knopf) and Barbara Zimmerman (later Barbara Epstein), who became the founder of *The New York Review of Books*. Both of them became so engrossed in Anne's journal that they couldn't put it down. They saw in the words of a young girl a universal cry against injustice and a message of mutual tolerance. Thanks to the efforts of these two editors, Anne's diary got the chance to reach tens of millions of readers across the world for generations to come. I hope that her words will continue to touch us, reminding us that ethics should rise above politics and that the values that unite us as human beings are far more important than the differences that divide us as groups.

Conclusion

Judaic Studies and the Holocaust via Reviews

As I conclude this book about the Holocaust, it's only natural to reflect about the main discipline such a project pertains to: namely, the field of Judaic Studies. In what follows I'd like to describe what "Judaic Studies" means to me and how it ties into the approach I pursued in presenting the Holocaust through a series of reviews of memoirs, histories, novels and films on the subject.

1. *Diversity*. In my estimation, Judaic Studies is more about intellectual and ethnic affinities, a wide-ranging curiosity, and the willingness to learn from one another than about having a common religious identity. The Jewish people themselves come from nearly every culture and civilization; speak almost every language on Earth; range widely in religious background (from deeply observant Orthodoxy to secular Judaism), and have no agreed-upon political views. And yet, for thousands of years they have felt affinities with each other and been united in a strong yet mysterious "family resemblance," or a series of overlapping connections and similarities, to use Wittgenstein's term.

2. *Centripetal and centrifugal cultural forces*. Judaic Studies therefore is not about manifesting or seeking an ethnic essence or unified cultural and religious identity. This makes sense, especially given the fact that, as history has shown, to be discriminated against on the basis of your "Judaism" you don't have to have Jewish parents or religious beliefs. According to Hitler's Nuremberg Laws, a "Jew" was a person who had three or four Jewish grandparents. This tenet cast a wide net of

discrimination. One of my favorite painters, Marc Chagall, who was Jewish, was obliged between the years 1941–1948 to escape from occupied France to the United States once the Nazi regime took over his country. But so was Vladimir Nabokov, the prize-winning Russian author. Nabokov was not Jewish, but he expressed sympathy for the plight of the Jews. That was enough to endanger his life. I am drawn to what I'd describe as a simultaneous push and pull, or the centrifugal and centripetal forces, that exist in a hybrid field like Judaic Studies. There's a force away from any set identity or even agreed-upon religious core yet, at the same time, an attraction to Jewish culture, religion and achievements that span countries and centuries.

3. *Manifest curiosity about all fields without claiming to master them.* To write a work pertaining to the field of Judaic Studies, you don't have to know everything about Jewish cultures and religion. That would be an impossible task. How can anyone know everything about thousands of years of such heterogeneous cultures and traditions? Besides, nowadays, nobody can become Encyclopedic in the way the philosophes were during the Enlightenment. There's no way anyone can be familiar with thousands of years of Jewish history; the vast transformations in Judaism and its religious and cultural practices; the multiplicity of languages spoken by Jews (aside from Hebrew and Yiddish); the immense contributions that both Jews and those who are interested in Judaism have made in every field of human knowledge. Approaching the dark epoch of the history of European Jews during WWII through the prism of reviews has enabled me to interweave general historical information with the particular documents—memoirs, histories, novels and films—about the Holocaust that I found most valuable and illuminating. In this way, I aim to offer a broad study of the Holocaust without claiming to have either the comprehensiveness or the strict, alphabetical, organization of an Encyclopedia. My approach in writing this book was inspired by the original sense of the sixteenth-century notion of *enkuklios paideia*, meaning an "all-around education." By starting with individual works about the Holocaust and incorporating historical information about WWII, *Holocaust Memories: A Survey of Holocaust Memoirs, Histories, Novels, and Films* offers high school and college students, as well as teachers and the general reader, the *starting point* of a well-rounded education about this catastrophe—one that will hopefully be deepened and enriched by reading (or viewing) the sources I introduced here.

4. *The Holocaust and Judaic Studies.* Any study of the Holocaust is central to the field of Judaic Studies because it pertains to the darkest epoch in Jewish history, when the Jews were targeted for discrimina-

tion, deportation, and eventually extermination precisely for being Jewish. In *The Origins of Totalitarianism*, Hannah Arendt emphasizes that although other groups were also targeted by the Nazi regime for extermination—for example, the Gypsies, the Poles and Russian prisoners of war—it was not accidental that the extermination of Jews throughout Europe and, if possible, in the entire world was Hitler's top priority. And yet, in my reviews, I also pointed out that the Holocaust is not a subject that is relevant only to the Jews or that pertains only to the discipline of Judaic Studies. While having particular relevance to the Jewish people, it is at the same time a subject with universal, human significance. As Primo Levi states in *The Drowned and The Saved*, "It happened, therefore it can happen again."

5. *Other genocides*. Whatever complex historical conditions made it possible to dehumanize, ostracize, and kill millions of people could occur again, in a similar manner, against the Jews or other groups. The only way to address these atrocities is by acknowledging them, learning about them and doing our best to avoid them now and in the future. This begins, on an existential level, with saying "No" to even the first step of dehumanizing groups of people in order to discriminate against and harm them.

6. *Preserving collective memories of the Holocaust*. The books and films I reviewed in *Holocaust Memories* offer us vivid reminders about where the process of dehumanization can lead and how it impacts individuals, not statistics. It's unfortunately too easy to depersonalize suffering when considering it on such a massive, almost unfathomable scale.

The way most of the victims perished—often shot en masse or gassed after being subjected to extraordinary cruelty and abuse—was in itself, quite deliberately, an abject form of dehumanization. The narratives and films I have reviewed in this book emphasize the value of each of the millions of human beings who suffered and perished during the Holocaust.

Bibliography

Ancel, Jean. *The History of the Holocaust in Romania*. Jerusalem: Yad Vashem, 2011.
Appleman-Jurman, Alicia. *Alicia: My Story*. New York: Bantam Books,1990.
Arendt, Hannah. *The Origins of Totalitarianism*. San Diego: Harcourt, Inc., 1948.
Auerbacher, Inge. *I Am a Star: Child of the Holocaust*. New York: Puffins Books, 1986.
Babiak, Paul and Hare, Robert D. *Snakes in Suits: When Psychopaths Go to Work*. New York: Harper Collins, 2006.
Balakian, Peter. T*he Burning Tigris: The Armenian Genocide and America's Response*. New York: Harper Perennial, 2004.
Bannister, Nonna. *The Secret Holocaust Diaries*. New York: Tyndale House Publishers, 2009.
Barnes, Julian. *The Noise of Time: A Novel*. Knopf: New York, 2016.
Beevor, Antony. *The Second World War*. New York: Little, Brown & Company, 2012.
Berg, Mary. *The Diary of Mary Berg: Growing Up in the Warsaw Ghetto*. New York: Oneworld Publications, 2009.
Blumental Lazan, Marion, and Perl, Lila. *Four Perfect Pebbles, A Holocaust Story*. New York: Scholastic, 1996.
Brent, Jonathan, and Naumov Vladimir. *Stalin's Last Crime: The Plot against the Jewish Doctors*, 1948–1953. New York: HarperCollins eBooks, 2010.
Browning, R. Christopher. *Ordinary Men: Reserve Police Battalion 101 and the Final Solution in Poland*. New York: Harper Perennial, 1993.
Bing, S. *What Would Machiavelli Do?* New York: Harper Collins, 2000.
Black, D., and C. Larson, *Bad Boys, Bad Men: Confronting Antisocial Personality Disorder*. Oxford: Oxford University Press, 2000.
Bitton-Jackson, Livia. *I Have Lived a Thousand Years: Growing Up in the Holocaust*. New York: Simon Pulse, 1999.
Blair, James. *The Psychopath: Emotion and the Brain*. New York: Wiley-Blackwell, 2005.
Bornstein, Michael, and Debbie. *Survivors Club: The True Story of a Very Young Prisoner of Auschwitz*. New York: Farrar, Straus and Giroux, 2017.
Boyne, John. *The Boy in the Striped Pajamas*. New York: Random House, 2006.
Brown, Daniel James. *The Boys in the Boat: Nine Americans and Their Epic Quest for Gold at the 1936 Berlin Olympic*s. New York: Penguin Books, 2014.
Bullock, Alan. *Hitler and Stalin: Parallel Lives*. New York: Vintage Edition, 1991.
Chang, Iris. *The Rape of Nanking: The Forgotten Holocaust of WWII*. New York: Penguin Books, 1997.
Cleckley, Hervey. *The Mask of Sanity*, fifth edition. St. Louis: Mosby, 1976.
Cohn Dekel, Sheila, and Lucette Matalon Lagnado. *Children of the Flames*. New York: Penguin Books, 1992.

Conquest, Robert. *Reflections on a Ravaged Century*. New York: Norton, 2000.
Conquest, Robert. *The Great Terror: A Reassessment*. Oxford: Oxford University Press, 1990.
Deletant, Dennis. *Hitler's Forgotten Ally: Ion Antonescu and His Regime, Romania 1940–1944*. New York: Palgrave MacMillan, 2006.
Demick, Barbara. *Nothing to Envy: Ordinary Lives in North Korea*. New York: Spiegel and Grau, Random House, 2009.
De Rosnay, Tatiana. *Sarah's Key: A Novel*. New York: St. Martin's Griffin, 2008.
Dikotter, Frank. *Mao's Great Famine: The History of China's Most Devastating Catastrophe, 1958-1962*. New York: Walker and Company, 2011.
Doblert, Duane L. *Understanding Personality Disorders: An Introduction*. Connecticut: Praegar Publishers, 2007.
Edsel, Robert M. *The Monuments Men: Allied Heroes, Nazi Thieves and the Greatest Treasure Hunt in History*. New York: Center Street, 2010.
Frank, Anne. *The Diary of a Young Girl*. New York: Bantam Books, 1993.
Ginsburg, Eugenia. *Journey into the Whirlwind*. New York: Mariner Books, 2001.
Gutman, Israel. *Resistance*. New York: Houghton Mifflin, *1994*, 99.g
Hare, Robert D. *Psychopathy: Theory and Research*. New York: Wiley; Gordon Trasler, 1978.
Hillenbrand, Laura. *Unbroken*, New York: Random House, 2010.
Holland, Travis. *The Archivist's Story*. New York: Bantam Books, 2007.
Filderman, Wilhelm, Edited by Jean Ancel. *Memoirs and Diaries*. Jerusalem: Yad Vashem, 2004.
Hansen, Ron. *Hitler's Niece*. New York: Harper Collins, 1999.
Hare, Robert D. *Manual for the Revised Psychopathy Checklist*, 2nd Edition. Toronto, Ontario: Multi-Health Systems, 2003.
Hare, Robert D. *Without Conscience: The Disturbing World of the Psychopaths Among Us*. New York: Guilford Press, 1998.
Harrowitz, Nancy. *Tainted Greatness: Antisemitism and Cultural Heroes*. Philadelphia: Temple University Press, 1994.
Hastings, Max. *Inferno, the World at War 1939–1945*. New York: Random House, 2012.
Herling, Gustaw. *A World Apart: Imprisonment in a Soviet Labor Camp During World War Two*. New York: Penguin Books, 1996.
Hilberg, Raul. *The Destruction of the European Jews*. New York: Holmes and Meyer Publishers, 1985.
Hilberg, Raul. *Perpetrators, Victims, Bystanders: The Jewish Catastrophe 1933–1945*. New York: HarperCollins Publishers, 1992.
Hitler, Adolf, Translated by James Murphy. *Mein Kampf*. London: Hurst and Blackett Publishers, 1939.
Ioanid, Radu. *The Holocaust in Romania*. Chicago: Ivan R. Dee, 2000.
Jeffreys, Diarmuid. *Hell's Cartel: IG Farben and the Making of Hitler's War Machine*. New York: Henry Holt and Company, 2008.
Jiang, Ji-li. *Red Scarf Girl*. New York: HarperCollins, 2004.
Judt, Tony. *Postwar: A History of Europe since 1945*. New York: Penguin Books, 2005.
Kanton, Martin. *The Psychopathy of Everyday Life: How Antisocial Personality Disorder Affects All of Us*. Connecticut: Praegar Publishers, 2006.
Kernberg, Otto. *Borderline Conditions and Pathological Narcissism*. New York: Jason Aronson, 1985.
Keneally, Thomas. *Shindler's List*. New York: Simon and Shuster, 1982.
Kershaw, Alex. *The Envoy*. New York: Da Capo Press, 2010.
Kershaw, Ian. *Hitler: A Biography*. New York: W. W. Norton & Company, 2010.
Kertesz, Imre. *Fatelessness*. New York: Vintage Interantional, 2004.
Koker, David. *At the Edge of the Abyss: A concentration Camp Diary* 1943–1944. Edited by Robert Jan van Pelt. Evanston: Northwestern University Press, 2012.
Korczak, Janusz. *Ghetto Diary*. New Haven: Yale University Press, 2003.
Levi, Primo. *Moments of Reprieve: A Memoir of Auschwitz*. New York: Penguin Books, 1985.
Levi, Primo. *Survival in Aushwitz*. New York: Touchstone, 1996.
Levi, Primo. *The Drowned and the Saved*. New York: Vintage International, 1989.

Levi, Primo. *The Reawakening*. New York: Touchstone, 1995.
Levy, Alan. *Nazi Hunter: The Wiesenthal File*. New York: Barnes and Noble Books, 1993.
Lewy, Guenter. *The Nazi Persecution of the Gypsies*. Oxford: Oxford University Press, 2001.
Lifton, Betty Jean. *The King of Children: A Biography of Janusz Korczac*. New York: Farrar, Straus and Giroux, 1988.
Lifton, Robert Jay. *The Nazi Doctors: Medical Killing and the Psychology of Genocide*. New York: Basic Books, 1988.
Lindner, Robert. *Rebel Without a Cause*. New York: Grune and Straton, 1944.
Lindwer, Willy. *The Last Seven Months of Anne Frank*. New York: Double Day, 1988.
Lowen, Alexander. *Narcissism: Denial of the True Self*. New York: Macmillan, 1983.
Lykken, David T. New York: *The Antisocial Personalities*, Lawrence Erlbaum, 1995.
Lyotard, Jean-François. *The Postmodern Condition: A Report on Knowledge*. Minnesota: University of Minnesota Press, 1984.
Maier, Ruth. Translated by Jamie Bulloch. *Ruth Maier's Diary: A Jewish girl's life in Nazi Europe*. New York: Vintage, 2010.
Marton, Kati. *Wallenberg: The Incredible True Story of the Man Who Saved the Jews of Budapest*. New York: Arcade Publishing, 2011.
Minsky, Ruth. *The Cage*. New York: Simon & Shuster, 1997.
Muller, Philip. *Eyewitness Auschwitz: Three Years in the Gas Chambers*. Chicago: Ivan R. Dee, 1979.
Noakes, Jeremy, and Geoffrey Pridham, editors. *Nazism 1919–1945, Volume I*. Liverpool: Liverpool University Press, University of Exeter Series, 1998.
Orwell, George. *Homage to Catalonia*. New York: Mariner Books, 1980.
Orwell, George. *1984*, New York: Signet Classics, 1950.
Patrick, Christopher D., editor. *Handbook of Psychotherapy*. New York: The Guilford Press, 2007.
Peterson, Scott. *Me Against My Brother*. New York: Routledge, 2000.
Polak, Joseph. *After the Holocaust the Bells Still Ring*. New York: Urim Publications, 2015.
Pressburger, Chava, Editor. Petr Ginz. *The Diary of Petr Ginz 1941–1942*. New York: Grove Press, 2004.
Prose, Francine. *Anne Frank: The Book, the Life, the Afterlife*. New York: Harper Collins, 2009.
Reid, William H. *Unmasking the Psychopath: Antisocial Personality and Related Syndromes*. New York: W. W. Norton, 1986.
Rene, Alice. *Becoming Alice: A Memoir*. Iuniverse, 2008.
Ryan, Allan A. *Quiet Neighbors*. New York: Harcourt Brace Jovanovich, 1984.
Schuessler, Jennifer. "Survivor Who Hated the Spotlight." New York Times, November 10, 2014.
Segev, Thomas. *Soldiers of Evil*. Jerusalem: Domino Press, 1987.
Sebastian, Mihai. *Journal 1935–1944: The Fascist Years*. New York: Ivan R. Dee Publishers, 2000.
Stangneth, Bettina. *Eichmann Before Jerusalem: The Unexamined Life of a Mass Murderer*. New York: Random House, 2014.
Styron, William. *Sophie's Choice*. New York: Vintage International, 1976, 1992.
Szpilman, Wladyslaw. *The Pianist*. New York: Picador Press, 1999.
Stargardt, Nicholas. *Witnesses of War: Children's Lives Under the Nazis*. New York: Vintage Books, 2007.
Staub, Ervin. *The Roots of Evil: The Origins of Genocide and Other Group Violence*. Cambridge: Cambridge University Press, 1989.
Stout, Martha. *The Sociopath Next Door*. New York: Broadway Books, 2005.
Tismaneanu, Vladimir. *Stalinism for All Seasons: A Political History of Romanian Communism*. Berkeley: University of California Press, 2003.
Tusa, Ann, and John Tusa. *The Nuremberg Trial*. New York: Atheneum, 1986.
Tuvel Bernstein, Sara. *The Seamstress: A Memoir of Survival*. New York: Penguin Group, 1997.
Wiesel, Elie. *Night*. New York: Hill and Wang, 2006.

Bibliography

Wiesenthal, Simon. *The Sunflower: On the Possibilities and Limits of Forgiveness*. New York: Schocken Books, 1998.
Wladyslaw, Szpilman. *The Pianist*. New York: Picador Press, 1999.
Wolman, Benjamin B. *Antisocial Behavior: Personality Disorders from Hostility to Homicide*. New York: Prometheus Books, 1999.
Yahil, Leni. *The Holocaust: The Fate of European Jewry, 1932–1945*, translated from Hebrew by Ina Friedman and Haya Galai. Oxford: Oxford University Press, 1990.
Zusak, Markus. *The Book Thief*. New York: Albert A. Knopf, 2007.

About the Author

Claudia Moscovici earned an AB in Comparative Literature from Princeton University and a PhD in Comparative Literature (with a focus on French Enlightenment and Romanticism) from Brown University. She is the author of the critically acclaimed novels *Velvet Totalitarianism* (2009) and *The Seducer* (2011). *Velvet Totalitarianism* was republished in translation in her native country, Romania, under the title *Intre Doua Lumi* (Curtea Veche Publishing, 2011). In 2002, she co-founded with Mexican sculptor Leonardo Pereznieto the international aesthetic movement called "postromanticism," devoted to celebrating beauty, passion and sensuality in contemporary art. She wrote a book on Romanticism and its postromantic survival called *Romanticism and Postromanticism* (Lexington Books, 2007) and taught literature, philosophy, and arts and ideas at Boston University and at the University of Michigan. She also published a nonfiction book on predatory relationships called *Dangerous Liaisons* (Rowman & Littlefield Publishing, 2011), which has been translated into Italian under the title *Relazioni Pericolose* (Edizioni Sonda, 2017) and launched at the Feltrinelli bookstore in Rome and at the Italian Parliament.

www.ingramcontent.com/pod-product-compliance
Lightning Source LLC
Chambersburg PA
CBHW020123240426
43673CB00038B/571